"The dull man, who had tried to put [Oscar] Wilde out of countenance, suddenly said to the whole room, roused by I cannot remember what incautious remark meant for the man at my side, ,Yeats believes in magic; what nonsense!' Henley said, 'No, it may not be nonsense; black magic is all the rage in Paris now'. And then turning towards me with a changed sound in his voice, 'It is just a game, isn't it?'"

(William Butler Yeats, approx. 1896, Nobel Prize in Literature 1923)

"Spiritualism, indeed, necessarily attracted within its sphere the 'cranks', the social theorists and reformers, the rebels against convention and the exiles from society."

(Frank Podmore, natural scientist, †1910)

"Personal freedom which indeed exists is perhaps important on an individual basis. From a cosmological perspective it is nothing. Orders seem to be given; agents that have tremendous power seem to acknowledge them. Human beings execute them like theater puppets ... There are angels of light and angels of darkness. At a certain point it is necessary to choose sides."

(Jean Marquès-Rivière, French SS-Collaborateur, 1929)

Séance with the Italian medium Eusapia, hovering table and du Prel (holding her knee).
Himmler wrote in 1923 about a book of du Prel's:
"A small scientific work on a philosophical basis which truly has me believing in spiritualism and was the first to really introduce me to it."
(Bundesarchiv (German Federal Archives), Himmler, Leseliste (Reading list), P. 20)

Franz Wegener

# Heinrich Himmler

German Spiritualism,
French Occultism
and the
Reichsführer-SS

Translated by Herbert Windolf
Edited by Zene Krogh,
except for Footnotes
"The Caftan" edited by Lynn Chesson

KFVR

Wegener, Franz:
Heinrich Himmler
German Spiritualism, French Occultism and the Reichsführer-SS
Gladbeck/Germany: KFVR - Kulturförderverein Ruhrgebiet e.V.,
Second Edition 2013
Series: Political Religion of National Socialism: 4) The Ether

A heartfelt thank you to: Lynn Chesson, Werner Habel, Sabine Kettler, Zene Krogh, Stefan Laurin, Eva-Maria Stuckel and Herbert Windolf.

© 2013 Franz Wegener. All Rights Reserved. No part of this work may be reproduced, modified, reproduced or circulated in any form without written permission of the author.

http://www.franz-wegener.de
http://www.kfvr.de
Cover Design: buchgestaltung.de
Cover photo: E007485 © Getty Images
Logo KFVR: Frank Lucas
Printing: *CreateSpace Independent Publishing Platform*, USA
ISBN 978-1489514332

**Citations P. 1**

1) Yeats, 288. James Webb about Yeats: „*From the traditions of occult Masonry, with its attempt to duplicate the ecstatic effects of the ancient Mysteries, and a hybrid of ritual magic and the Cabala, S.L. MacGregor Mathers and Dr. Wynn Westcott concocted [1888] in England 'the Order of the Golden Dawn' to which belonged, at various times, Florence Farr the actress, Aleister Crowley and, notably, W.B. Yeats.*" [Webb, Underground, 275]

2) Podmore, Frank (1856-1910): *Modern Spiritualism. A History and a Criticism*, vol. II, p. 293, London 1902 (zit. n. Webb, *Underground*, 352)

3) Bhotiva, 25ff.

# Content

1 Kurt Münzer: The Caftan — 7

2 Tabular Curriculum vitae of Heinrich Himmler — 15

**3 Foreword — 17**

4 The female Demon: The fly-like Epidemic Witch Nasav — 25

5 The Spirits: Du Prel, Jürgens, Fidler, zur Bonsen, Heise — 37

6 The Stars: Wilhelm Wulff — 67

7 The Paranoia: Baron Gotthard von der Osten-Sacken — 71

8 The Polars: Maurice Magre, Jean-Marqués-Rivière, Gaston de Mengel — 77

**9 Afterword — 139**

10 Bibliography — 147

11 Index — 155

Illustration by Alfred Kubin (1877-1959) to the Narration
"The Caftan" by Kurt Münzer

# 1 Kurt Münzer: The Caftan

A Short Story from 1915
Read by Himmler in 1922

Our charitable transport was returning. We had taken all kinds of good supplies to the front and were driving home in six cars, I in the last. It was a dreary January day, at noon already as dark as evening, but then it once more was slowly brightening. The monotonous gray sky turned to clouds which were gradually moving north. A dull silver broke through, and right away the snow answered with sparkle and light.

We left a hilly valley, a sparse forest, into which sounded the growl of artillery. Then, the hillocks behind us rose like barriers through which no sound penetrated any more. When we rushed down into the white, empty, depressing Galizian plain, it became deathly quiet around us. Only the hammering and chuffing of our motors created a hellish noise in the empty world.

The sun was setting. Suddenly, pink broke through the clouds covering the entire western sky. The day did not pass as a blazing torch, but as a red-gold beacon, tender and sweet, like a girl's blush or a child's smile. An inexpressibly delicate pink streamed from the sky, the gray clouds becoming violet. All shades of lilac performed there a symbolic symphony. Young love, chaste dreams, tender longing – all were expressed by this final hour of the day. And the land below this sky responded. There were only the plain, sparse woods, a dead village, a lone farmstead, all white, but all now glowing timidly and softly, rising like a deep, happy breath. Lifeless at first, the scene now seemed to swell with life. The melancholy that had rested on nature was lifting. Here, too, a smile crossed the world. Beauty strode through the war.

I slowed the rush of my machine, let the five cars ahead of me disappear faster and faster, and stayed behind. After the frightening experiences out there on the front, I longed for silence, peace, and beauty. Slowly traveling down the empty, straight road, I enjoyed this colorful hour. I no longer sensed the cold.

However, the sweet evening glow did not last long. It faded quickly and totally. A gray, sadder and heavier than before, descended. I became nervous, shivering, and trembling to the depth of my heart. I suddenly sensed how exhausted I was, hungry, cold to the bones, my mind full of bloody, painful images. I quickly dashed after my companions. The infinite loneliness around me suddenly frightened me. I engaged my fastest gear and the car leaped forward.

An empty, shot-up village, a wooden bridge, a beheaded Christ statue on a wrecked cross beside the path. A forest with screaming ravens, again the endless road, bare trees, white, icy shapes, then hillocks, hillocks, hillocks; a soldiers' cemetery, crosses, helmets, rifle pyramids, all snowed over. Where were the other cars? Had I caught up with them, they should long since have become visible to me on this flat plain. I did not see nor hear anything. And it was getting dark. I stopped to listen. Oh, how deathly silent everything was! It seemed as if I had entered the realm of the dead, a world that had lost its breath. No sound near or far.

Speeding, flying, leaping along. Another village without a shadow. A church, its tower shot off. I stop to light the car lantern. And now, in its light, I see the road ahead is without wheel tracks. No one has passed by here for an entire day. The snow from last night lies untouched before me. I have lost my way ...

I'm getting cold, as if ice water is flowing through my veins instead of blood. I look around. It is night. The sky is dark. Only the snow provides a dull glow. And my light carves a shiny section from this white, dead, empty world, which is more dreadful than the impenetrable darkness around me.

I am carrying no map. Did I not drive in the tracks of my companions? What should I do? Turn around and look for the right direction? Suddenly, I shudder, remembering what lay behind me. I sound the horn to signal into the night. How awful sounds this howl, as if a giant animal were crying for help or screaming from hunger. Silence. No reply. The silence only rests heavier on me, presses and chokes. This empty world appears infinite, with me the last living being. On, on! Somewhere, there must be a way out. I let the car surge ahead. Off, off! Away! Out of here!

Abruptly there is something: from the empty world grows a town, darker than the night, a pile of threatening black shapes in the white landscape. First some houses, fences, then streets. Nowhere lights. But the snow and my lights illuminate the walls, doors, and windows. The buildings gape as if after an earthquake; furniture is tossed onto the streets; there a barricade rises, coats and pants draped over it. Are there still people trapped inside, soldiers ... ? I turn away. There's a side street, just a passageway, deep in snow. I drive slowly. It is a dead town, shelled, stormed, abandoned. There's no one here, not even an animal. A square opens. There's a church that seems to topple; in the middle of the square a monument, a man with a single arm, the other shot off. Over there a rustle, a flutter, a whispering, and a flock of birds rises, larger, darker.

On I drive through narrow streets. There's a park with trees and bushes, a frozen pond. I keep seeing more. I see empty windows, from one hanging a curtain, gently waving. It is eerie, like a ghostly greeting. That something should move in this town! There's a fountain. A bowl, a tall figure on top, the once leaping waters frozen. White arcs wrap around, catching the reflection of my lights and arching like hammered silver.

Gradually becoming aware that I am probably dreaming, my fear also recedes. I only ask myself whether it can really be a dream, if I can call it that. But then the mood of this experience touches me so deeply that I no longer think about it, but simply accept it as reality without questioning.

Entire houses open their interior, for their walls fronting the street have collapsed. Iron staircases, tossed about, lie in the middle of the street. There, snowed in, rises the corpse of a horse, and over there I notice other dark shapes.

I get out of the car and walk toward them. Bodies. Women and men, a child. The last residents of the town. Perhaps they remained stubbornly, then starved and froze to death. I do not shudder. Everything becomes natural and obvious. I do not experience, I only see it. There, on a threshold someone sits. An old woman. She doesn't move when I touch her. She is dead but does not topple. She's frozen stiff. She smiles.

The snow illuminates the town. The night becomes brighter than the evening.

Then, two lights beckon to me from over there, green and fiery. A dog – lying on a threshold. A Moorish-Oriental house, lancet windows, the facade still standing. But behind, it has collapsed. In a window grating is the eye of God. It is the synagogue. And in front of the Jewish temple is the dog. He holds a boot between his paws, gnawed to the soles, nails protruding from the leather. He cannot eat more without tearing up his muzzle. He is a large, shaggy animal, like a wolf. Maybe he is one? He bares his teeth, raises his head towards me. But he can no longer get up. Weakened, he lies there dying, and guarding – what?

Then I hear it. Behind the door, inside the destroyed temple, a murmur, singing, whispering. A single voice, rising and lowering, wild, fanatical, ardent.

I push over the threshold. The dog mutters the echo of a growl. He protects his master. For in the anteroom of the synagogue, whose rear wall has collapsed, a person walks back and forth, a man.

I turn on my flashlight. Its bright cone catches the oldster in his long caftan. A Jew with gray temple locks under a little black skull cap, with a long-bearded, yellow face that looks chiseled from sulfur rock. He stands there, frozen, as if the sudden light has the power to transfix him. In his arms he carries a large scroll as he would a child, the Torah scroll. Perhaps he rescued it, grabbing the sacred relic from the temple under threat to his life. For behind him towers a chaotic pile of stones, blocks, and ashlars. In the beam from my flashlight a metal candelabra sparkles through a break, there lies a piece of marble, a scrap of cloth with woven symbols.

And the old man, awoken from his transfixation, keeps on walking. He murmurs and sings a litany, incomprehensible and monotonous. Russian or Hebrew. He no longer pays attention to me, prays, holds the sacred scroll like a beloved pressed onto himself, and strides back and forth.

I step in his way; he does not react but keeps on walking. I call to him. He does not answer. His eyes are staring, they do not see nor grasp anything. He is likely emotionally blind and deaf. He is insane ...

For how long has he been wandering here and praying? His last conscious act may have been the rescue of the Torah scroll. Once it was in his hands, his spirit became confused. He has forgotten hunger and overcome the cold by his endless wandering. He has survived the death of his town. And his dog cannot die as long as his master lives.

I pursue him with the beam of my flashlight. But he does not mind it. His consciousness is impenetrable, otherworldly; I do not reach inside.

I shudder as if from something extrasensory. Everything inside me cramps up. This winter's night, the abandoned town with its dead, the dying dog, the insane Jew with his praying, droning voice in the wrecked temple . . .

But I get a hold of myself. I stop the old man. Whether he understands me or not, I tell him to come with me. I cannot leave him here, left to cold and hunger. I must save him, take him along to people to be cared for. Love wells up in me, as if this oldster were the last living being except for myself. From him emanates warmth, courage, stimulating me. I grasp him tightly as if he were the one who would save me. I must have a goal, a purpose, to get away from here. Otherwise, I feel I will remain here myself among the dead in this forlorn world, starve, freeze to death, or become insane ... I, I must get away, and the Jew must save me.

He does not answer, wants to pull himself away; he does not understand anything, may not even hear anything. I scream into his face. He remains stiff, uncomprehending, otherworldly. But I know this means death or life for him and me. Already, the spell of the dead town overcomes me. Invisible claws reach for me. A peculiar lethargy takes hold of me.

I pick up the oldster in my arms. He is feather-light, as if I were lifting an empty dress. And he is cold as ice. The scroll slips off and hits the floor with a dull sound. That is when he awakes and screams shrilly like a kicked dog. He hits my face, tears at my shoulders. But I carry him away. At the threshold the dog howls, feebly, with a rattle, as if he were dying. He drags himself, creeps after me; me, who is taking his master away.

There, in the middle of the street, stands my car. Its bright, golden light illuminates the lane. Just seeing it, warmth envelops me, and I find strength and courage. I carry the old man to the car and seat him inside. He no longer struggles against me. He collapses into himself like an empty coat. His hair and beard droop, hard, stiff. An odor emanates from him like decomposition.

I look for the dog. He lies three paces away, dead.

I crank up the engine, jump into the car and drive off. Only to be away, no matter to where. On, on! Somewhere I must find people. What if they are enemies? At least people! I am becoming insane in this solitude, death surrounding me, insanity behind. I don't dare to turn around to look at my passenger.

I race away as if I were fleeing from him.

And the town flies past me, houses, fences, barns, a boulevard, fields, more fields, all glittering white. Biting wind amidst whose knives I race ahead. Am I bleeding? And where does the road lead? A forest, shadows flitting past, dogs, wolves? A leap across a bridge. You magnificent engine, panting, brave, untiring! Again, an infinite world, empty, into which we greedily race. Then, a shout –

A shout where there had been a shadow; I am past, a shot sounds, something sings by me, a bullet. Halt! Stop! Stop! The car almost overturns. A sentry comes running. Germans! In ten minutes there will be a village and soldiers, staff headquarters. The name? Well known. There, we planned to stop over, us six cars. I have found the right way.

On the village square they wait, fearful, worried. Rejoicing surrounds me. It is ten o'clock. Two hours I was under way, longer than the others. Ah, light, the smell of food, people, talk, life, warmth.

I want to lift my Jew from the car. There, he lies on the seat, unmoving. I reach for him – and hold an empty caftan in my hand ...

Men stare at me, waiting. I look around, terrified. The caftan is empty. No body is inside. I shake it as if the Jew would come tumbling out.

I am taken to a warm room and I tell my story. There's a map lying on the table; a young lieutenant searches and searches. But in the entire area there's no town, neither near nor far, only small villages. But I did not dream it, for there is the caftan! The caftan!

Insulted, I refuse to take the medicinal powder the regimental doctor wants to give me. I get the promise to be accompanied the next day, to follow my tire tracks and to look for the dead town. But, during the night it snows and snows, and by next morning all is covered. Nothing tells where I came from.

We drive home. There's the caftan. And since it smells of decay, I throw it away. Now, the last proof of my experience is gone. Experience! For it was no dream. From what dream does one carry material things into life? I cannot explain it. But maybe the oldster jumped from the car, leaving the caftan behind, to return to his sacred role and his dead brothers. Maybe ...[1]

---

[1] from: Eulenberg, Herbert, et al.: Der Gespensterkrieg [The Ghost War], Stuttgart 1915, P. 77-85

Heinrich Himmler (1900-1945)

# 2 Tabular Curriculum vitae of Heinrich Himmler

| | |
|---|---|
| October 7, 1900 | Born in Munich as son of of the gymnasium teacher and princely educator Gebhard Himmler |
| Jan.-Dec. 1918 | Military training |
| 1919-1922 | Study at the TH Munich |
| August 1, 1922 | Agricultural master's exam |
| Sept. 1922 - Aug. 1923 | Technical assistant with the Stickstoff-Land GmbH, Schleißheim |
| 1919–1923 | Paramilitary service with the Free-corps "Alarm-Kompanie," Residents defence "Reichskriegsflagge" |
| August 1923 | Entry into the NSDAP |
| November 1923 | Participation in the November Putsch |
| 1925 | Assistant Gauleiter in Lower Bavaria |
| 1926 | Assistant Gauleiter in Upper Bavaria; Assistant Reichspropagandaleiter |
| 1927 | Assistant Reichsführer-SS (Entry into the SS 1926, Member No. 168) |
| Juli 1928 | Marriage |
| January 1929 | Reichsführer-SS |
| 1930 | Member of the Reichstag |
| April 1933 | Commander of the Bavarian political police; Police president of Munich |
| June 17, 1936 | Chief of German police |
| October 7, 1939 | Reichskommissar for the Strengthening of German Tradition |
| 15 August 1943 | Reichsminister of the Interior and Plenipotentary for Administration of the Reich |
| 21 Juli 1944 | Supreme Commander of the Reserve (or Replacement) Army (Home, Ersatzheer) and Head of Military Armament |
| Dec. 10, 44–Jan. 23, 45 | Supreme Commander of Army Group Oberrhein |
| Jan. – March 1945 | Supreme Commander of Army Group Weichsel |
| May 23, 1945 | Suicide in British Imprisonment[1] |

---

1  Tabular overview following Loenartz, Marianne: "Nachlaß Heinrich Himmler (1900-1945)," Publication of the Bundesarchiv (German Federal Archives), Koblenz 2003, page III

Grave of Gérard Encausse whose esoteric pseudonym was Papus; cemetery Père-Lachaise, Paris (photo: Franz Wegener, 2006)

# 3 Foreword

The Paris of the nineteenth century was then the world's California. And the master of French spiritualism, Papus, was somewhat like today's founder of Apple, Steve Jobs.[1] In this witches' cauldron, new approaches to life and fashions were continuously discovered, invented, tested, and again rejected. The transitions between alchemy and chemistry were still fluid, and those between spiritualism, Mesmerism, hypnosis and psychology, as well. The French Revolution was an event the memory of which was still fresh. Likewise, one was aware of the beginning loss of significance of the Church. The emerging vacuum was taken advantage of by several movements, among which was Theosophy, which concluded from William Jones' discovery on a common Indo-European language family a once-existing, common primeval religion; wanting to return to this very "Urreligion" through a synthesis of the world's religions. The contact with Asian religions revived memories of the old and familiar: The medieval heretics' movement of the Katharer bore numerous features of the newly discovered religions from the other end of the world. And these associations were by no means wrong. The gnostic heretics inspired by the Bulgarian Bogumiles, in turn went back to the Paulicans in Constantinople, who profited themselves from the earlier counter designs of Mani. Mani had already attempted – at times very successfully – what Helena Blavatsky would try hundreds of years later anew: To develop a synthesis of East and West. He fused the Christian point of view with Zoroastic and Indian rituals, as well as Buddhist philosophy.[2] As a result of this convergence of old and new most of the French occult groups, which will be addressed here, were marked by Gnosticism – some with more, some with less Christian, Hindu and Buddhist elements.

---

1  see: Wegener, Gnosis in High Tech und Science Fiction
2  Hergemöller about east-west religion transfer: "The numerous conspicuous parallels between the Tibetan Buddhism and the Lepzet articles [about a Middle Age heretic from Cologne, about 1231 who, in the interrogation text was assigned to the Manicheans / Katharers] (Predestination doctrine, predetermination of a boy, vegetarianism, transmigration of souls, koprophagy) cannot be attributed to direct connections between the Middle Age Buddhists and the European ‚heretics,' but rather to the power of attribution of antique authorities. (Distorted) characteristics of the Asian high religions did therefore arrive by the detour of (late) antique Persian and religious groups of Asia Minor, e.g., ‚Manicheans' or ‚Cataphryger,' as well as the patriotic polemic reacting to it to the Occident," [Hergemöller, 39, 50, 132]

James Webb, who died much too early, must be credited with being the first researcher who, with scientific criticism, examined the Occultism[1] of the nineteenth century, although he knew very well that even the scientifically-distanced occupation with this subject could mean the end of a scientific carrier. These contact fears of historical science vis-à-vis the subject of Occultism are, by no means, irrational, but can be perfectly well understood: The, as a rule, source-free editions of the subject in the 1960s and 70s, especially on the side of the French, and the tendency of new and old Right-Wing radicals attempting to idealize National-Socialism by the detour of NS-Occultism, explain the until now broad neglect of this subject by German historians. The sources of this subject field are generally poor: An "occult," that is a group of people operating in hiding, will hardly entrust protocols of their meetings to the city archives for the purpose of later historical editing. A further problem: Even the witnesses of this milieu of the times, who, against expectation took a position in book form, often tended to conspiratorical fantasies and exaggerations. For instance, in contemporary literature one often finds references to secret service activities of the Occultists. In this connection, the historian is faced with the problem: Can the statements in the one or the other case be justified? They are rarely verifiable, since secret service organizations generally tend not to respond to inquiries regarding potential agents of their own. A further problem may rest in the personality of the scientist himself: In view of his own, early-morning look at the horoscope listings in the daily newspaper, one or the other reader may feel threatened by the possibility of his own relapse into magical modes of thinking, a threat to which he may react with dissociation. Accordingly, the dissociation towards scientists who had carried out this regression, were therefore already substantial in the twenties: This is why in 1921 a concerned scholar wrote: "Today, the number of researchers already established in other areas, who have directed their work

---

1   Stutterheim: "Occultism refers to the ‚doctrine of hidden things' and is used since the appearance of the work De occulta philosophica by Agrippa of Nettersheim, from which the term Occultism is derived. Agrippa of Nettersheim (1486-1535) – actually Henricus Cornelius Agrippa, studied theologian, an doctor of law and medicine, is one of the universal scholars of the Renaissance. He occupied himself extensively with the as such designated ‚hermetic tradition' and reviewed Jewish as well as Greco-Egyptian secret science ... Magic enabled Agrippa access to the higher worlds and served for the recognition of God ... Until the end of the 17th century occultism belonged by no means to rejected and hidden knowledge, but to the knowledge of educated elites." [Stutterheim, 39, 41] "Spiritualism meant to get in touch with the spirits of deceased by means of séances of various kinds." [Stutterheim, 67]

to the occult field, is already substantial. Already, individual men turned to it in the eighties and nineties of the past century. Our older generation remembers the sensation, when one of the founders of astrophysics, C. F. Zoellner, and his friend, the creator of psycho-physics, G. Th. Fechner, as well as the excellent English physicist [William] Crookes, occupied themselves with the Media Slade and Home. All three of them claimed the reality of phenomena totally different from all previous physical experience."[1] Despite all the problems the subject brought with it, not to tackle it, raised several overall issues: first, to leave an exciting part of the history of ideas unaddressed, and second, to leave the field to those intending to pursue new right-wing politics using the occult.

At that, the subject can be addressed with little emotion. How James Webb defined the "Occult": "[Occupation with the Occultism of the nineteenth century is necessary,] to understand – to take a few examples – the components of early Nazism,[2] some directions in psychoanalysis, the rebellion of the hippies, or ... of flying saucers. ,The occult' has been defined as 'rejected knowledge.' This means that knowledge of a potentially valuable kind may be classified as 'occult' just as easily as knowledge once accepted but now discarded as primitive, facile, or simply mistaken."[3] It would be arrogant and wrong, too, to prematurely shove the occult-spiritualistic worlds of the nineteenth century into the drawer of the irrational. From the perspective of that time, it was unclear whether, after the diverse breathtaking discoveries, further different radiation types could still be demonstrated to exist, like the assumed body energy of the "Od."

---

1   Oesterreich, 23
2   The Himmler biographer Padfield wrote in 2000: "The war was not so much a rational war of conquest ... as an irrational, even a mystic revolution." [Padfield, xi] He demonized here National-Socialism – likely in contrast to the Christian image of man, and touched on the subject area of occultism/spiritualism only in passing, just like the Himmler expert Ackermann did later. [Padfield, 71; Ackermann, 34] Himmler biographer Peter Longerich 2010: "Central to Himmler's vision of the world was the restoration of a de-Christianized, Germanic environment, which with the help of the myths of Atlantis and Tibet was to be linked to long-lost examples of sophisticated cultures, and via the Cosmic Ice Theory / astrology /     astronomy to the history of the cosmos ... Through the mixture ... a real substitute religion was created ... His realization that the great majority of his fellow men would be unable – as yet – to recognize the intellectual consistency of his vision, and in particular that he would meet with vigorous opposition from Hitler should he, as one of the most important leaders of the NSDAP and Chief of the German Police, cause a stir by founding a substitute religion, made him cautious." [Longerich, 295f.]
3   Webb, Establishment, 15

Heinrich Himmler was born into a Catholic Family. His father was a princely educator and Gymnasium teacher. Young Heinrich was a strict believer and went regularly to mass, as can be seen from his diary.[1] However, with increasing age his spiritual interests shifted to new subjects areas. His religiosity began to drift and concentrated increasingly on the bizarre. Joachim Fest defines, as the essence of reading Himmler's speeches, the image of a man who, in the final consequence, was ruled by romantic-puerile dreams of Vikings.[2] Is it truly that trite? Are we truly dealing with a man who lived out that which pubescent boys play as a hobby? In the final analysis, we do not know what caused his break with the Church,[3] but the break had grave consequences. It created the vacuum into which Himmler could put his investigations for a new, great project: The creation of a new religion. We already meet at its beginnings this religion in National Socialism, a religion still *in statu nascendi:* in the state of its birth. Thus, as an example, Alfred Miller wrote in his anti-semitic "Manual for the Jewish Question": "The national revolution of the year 1933 did not leave a single area of religious or public life untouched ... Even if the religious revolution is still in its beginnings and is dragging all kinds of immature and halfcocked ideas along, ... nevertheless, the entire traditional substance of Church life had been, so to speak, put into question overnight."[4] This development points to

---

1     Ackermann, 21, 31
2     Fest, Joachim C.: Introduction to: Smith, 22
3     In concrete terms it possible dealt with fencing: "Behind the debate surrounding the so-called dueling question there was therefore an attempt on the part of the extreme right-wing students to enforce ethnic criteria throughout the network of student fraternities. The German-speaking fraternities in Austria had already denied Jews dueling status as a matter of principle in the 1890s, and after the end of the First World War radically anti-Semitic attempted to establish this principle throughout the fraternities. As a result Catholic members of fraternities experienced a fundamental conflict, as Catholic student organizations for reasons of principle resisted the marginalization of students of Jewish descent ... ,After dinner I had a conversation [...] about Jewishness, questions of honor and so on. A very interesting discussion. I was thinking about it on the way home. I think I am heading for conflict with my religion,' Himmler noted in his diary [1919] ..." [Longerich, 39f]
4     Miller, Alfred, article: "Die christlichen Kirchen und das Judentum – Die Wegbereiter der jüdischen Weltherrschaft", in: Fritsch, 244. According to Kersten, Himmler represented this position: "Everything is still in flux. We still wrestle ourselves for the final form. One can demand from adults that they participate in this struggle, even under the danger that they must, so to say, live along formlessly." [Kersten, 184] The hypothesis of the becoming religion is also represented by the Trimondis. [Trimondi, 17] However, I think their emphasis on far-eastern sources overweighed for this genesis. The new religion received

the fusion of two age-old, tried and tested, religious-philosophical movements: Cults of human sacrifice and Gnosis. The result: A gnostic cult of light, fired by permanent human sacrifices, motivated by a deep longing for the motherly origin. I have dedicated a book to each module of this imaginable synthesis: In "The Atlantis World View," I give evidence for the deep longing for Origin, based on the search of leading National Socialists and of New Rightists for the sunken continent Atlantis. Everything here revolves around the death-longing return to the mother imago and to the original element, water. In "Alfred Schuler, the last German Katharer," I demonstrate by a concrete example, the person of the Munich mentor of Stefan George, Alfred Schuler, the renaissance of Gnosis in the incubation phase of National Socialism. Here, the dominant model is light, from which the Gnostic believes he has originated, and whose divine part he believes to be, and to which he imagines returning. In the third volume of my series about the political religion of National Socialism, I finally occupy myself with the human sacrifices of National Socialism. Referencing the pre-Christian cults of human sacrifice by Germanic tribes, Celts and Slavic peoples, as well as the witch hunts of the Middle Ages and early modern times, I attempt to access the basic idea of human sacrifice in National Socialism. Standing in the the center of this exposition are the 'totally burned victims', the *holocausta*, to use a contemporary Italian term for the witch burnings of the early modern age – and that by fire. Water, light and fire – these are the leitmotifs from which my previous analysis of the political religion of National Socialism has been taken. The now available fourth volume of the series has, at its root, the motto of Ether,[1]

---

    its old patterns from gnostic traditions, which, originally possessed – also – a foundation in the far-eastern doctrine of salvation, but, in the Middle Ages in Europe, developed broadly autonomously, then via the Renaissance, Romantic, and the German Idealism became politically effective in National-Socialism. With the philological tapping of these religions, especially in the 19th century, although old affinities became obvious which were gratefully picked up by our European Gnostics, but they were largely accompanying fire of own European traditional forces.

1    In the Fin de Siècle Ether was defined as follows: "Ether, defined in Greek mythology as the personification of the upper, pure heavenly air, according to Hesiod, son of Erebos and the Night (Nyx), children of chaos; according to Hygin, next to the night, the day, and Erebos sired by chaos and the goddess of darkness (Caligio), as vice and evil arise from the union of Ether with the Earth of the Titans. According to both, the Ether appears as one of the basic substances from which the universe was built, but in the Orphyc Hymns represented as the world soul from which all life obtains its beginning and prosperity. Later, the Ether was imagined as being the celestial space, the abode of the gods, in which appears Zeus as its lord, who, dwelling in it was also imagined (as the son of Ether). – In

a mysterious element which, in the philosophy of antiquity and Middle Age alchemy, played a not insignificant role and points to the fringe elements of the researched *religio in statu nascendi:* Spiritualism and Occultism.

At that, it should be noted that all following statements to the political religion of National Socialism refer to the narrow exercise of a religio-philosophical investigation of National Socialism. Of course, such a movement cannot be explained monocausally. To it also belong social-historical causes, foreign policy aspects, individual, psychological factors, etc.

Foremost, Himmler and Alfred Rosenberg stood in the center of my research of the political religion of National Socialism – and not, as one might assume, Adolf

---

> Greek philosophy ether is the fifth element, filling the heavenly space, or the enlivening principle of warmth, imagined as artistic fire, from which all being, life, and thought originates. – In physics it is a fine, elastic substance filling the universe (World Ether) and the spaces between molecules of bodies, that must be assumed in order to explain the propagation of light, seen as a wave motion of the ether (light ether) ..." In [Meyers Konversations-Lexikon, 5th Edition, 2nd Volume, Leipzig 1894, P. 69], this physical definition was in 1950 already mute: "Physics: Light Ether is, following contemporary theory, an immaterial ... substance ..." ["Der kleine Brockhaus", Wiesbaden 1950, Vol. I, 73] Nowadays, ether is historically defined: "Ether ... quintessence (... *quinta essentia)*. Aristotle sees in Ether the expression with which the first humans called the divinity of the upper heaven ... Euripides, Zenon ... invoke the godhead in it ... Homer, Hesiod, the Orphicers, Pythagoreans, and Platonians imagine the Ether as being the heavenly light or as matter of a kind of light ... The Doxographs reported that Aristotle taught for souls to be of the same quintessence as stars; Kerakleides Pontikos declared the stuff of souls as etheric and the stars as a kind of light ... Syncretists melded the Ether doctrine of their predecessors to a kind of 'doctrina communis' and understood Ether as a type of light, animated, heavenly-astral, ethereally, most-fine matter. According to the new-Platonians, especially Porphyrio and Proklos, the bodies of demons and angels consist of it ... In the Renaissance the Ether appears as set above the other four elements, a heavenly-astral, invisible quintessence and as a medium between the spirit and body. Agrippa imagined this quintessence as a *'spiritus mundi'*: supposedly being a blossoming force and, simultaneously, principle of animation and change. Similarly, for Paracelsus all beings consist of an elementary, earthly, visible, and a heavenly, astral, invisible body, called *'spiritus'* ... According to Giordano Bruno, the Ether is boundless and animated, filling the universe and penetrates all bodies as 'spiritus universi' ... Newton [explained] the previous Ether-hypotheses from the physical position: the Ether, thought as being of finest matter, supposedly required to explain light and gravity manifestations. In the age of the Romantic ... the Ether theory experienced a renaissance. The ether-quintessence-idea is alive today, as it was earlier, especially in the teachings of the Vitalists, Theosophes, and Spiritualists." [Kurdzialek, Marian, article: "Ether, Quintessence," in: Ritter, Joachim (Ed.); "Historisches Wörterbuch der Philosophie" ["Historical Dictionary of Philosophy"], Vol. I, Basel 1971, column 599 ff.]

Hitler. Himmler, born in 1900, and Rosenberg were antipodes, yet, in the final consequence pursued the same goal: The building of a National-Socialistic world view which, in the light of the imagined destruction of Christian denominations in the post war time, had to culminate inevitably in a new German religion. To my knowledge, no active, constructive approaches for the creation of this new religion can be found in Hitler. Beyond this, Himmler, as Reichsführer-SS and master of concentration camps, the executive of mass murder, assumes a dissimilar yet more important position in the power structure of the system than Hitler did. Or, to speak with Lohalm/Scheffler: "Heinrich Himmler, who was often condescendingly smiled at because of his absurdity, and derisively called the 'Reichs Twerp', was in reality the forming power by which the Nationalist Socialist State with its crimes stands out in modern history."[1] This also suggests concentrating on the person and actions of Himmler in this volume.

At first, I will present several important personalities of German Spiritualism of the nineteenth century whose works impressed young Himmler very much. Already in the time of his service falls the promotion of the searcher for the Grail, Otto Rahn, and his turn toward Karl-Maria Wiligut, an Austrian Occultist, whom he put into a leading SS position. Since both persons have already been exhaustively dealt with,[2] they will be mentioned only briefly. Important for a psychogram of Himmler seems to me his reaction to the reading of the author, Baron von der Osten-Sacken who, obviously, was suffering from paranoia. Only this reaction makes it possible to explain what emerges in the chapter about the French occult scene of the twenties and its members' contacts with Himmler: the possible belief of the Reichsführer-SS of a worldwide conspiracy controlled by black magicians from the beyond against the powers of light – and the resulting political consequences.

This book no longer addresses the lure of a gnostic-inspired utopia of light-filled, blond, and bright-eyed Altantisers, but the other side of the strong dualism: The gnostic god of darkness and the fears emanating from it, fears, that motivated political decisions possibly even more strongly than the utopias of light were able to.

---

1  Himmler, Dienstkalender [Service calendar], Foreword, 9
2  Hans-Jürgen Lange has presented exceptional monographs to Rahn and Wiligut/Weisthor.

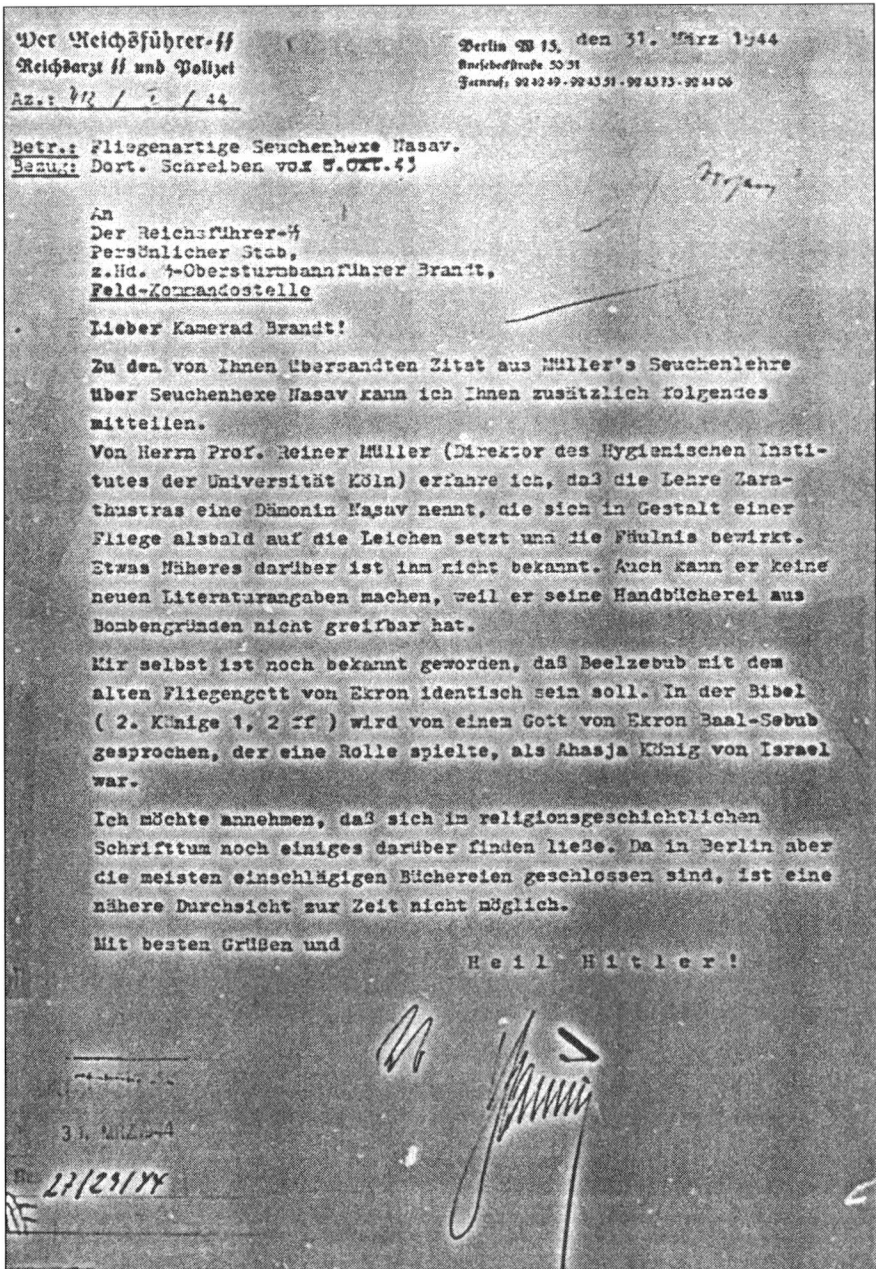

Letter of the SS Reichsarzt Ernst Grawitz to Brandt 1944 referencing the "Fly-like epidemic Witch Nasav" (German Federal Archives)

# 4 The female Demon: The fly-like Epidemic Witch Nasav

On March 31, 1944, the SS Reichs- and Police Doctor, Dr. Ernst Grawitz, wrote to the Reichsführer-SS (Field Command Position), attention SS Obersturmbannführer Brandt, the following letter:

Re.: Fly-like epidemic witch Nasav

"Dear Comrade Brandt!
Concerning the quotation you forwarded of Müller's Epidemic Doctrine about the Epidemic Witch Nasav, I can comment as follows:
I learned from Mr. Prof. Reiner Müller (Director of the Hygienic Institute of Cologne University) that Zarathustra's teachings name a female demon by the name of Nasav, which, in the manifestation of a fly, is quickly implanting herself on corpses to effect their decomposition. He is not aware of any further details. Also he cannot provide new literary references, his textbook library not being accessible due to bombing.
I myself have learned that Beelzebub is supposed to be identical with the old fly god Ekron. The Bible speaks of a god Ekron Baal-Sebub (Sec. Book of Kings, ch. 1, v. 2), who played some role when Ahasja was King of Israel.
I assume that more information may be found in the religio-historical literature. Since most relevant libraries in Berlin are closed, a more detailed checking is at present not possible.
With kind regards and
Heil Hitler!
Grawitz"[1]

With it, the SS Reichsdoctor reacted to Brandt's inquiry of October 8, 1943, wherein Müller's below quotation is found: "Professor Dr. Reiner Müller (Cologne), one of the most famous bacteriologists writes in his history of the causalities of epidemics: 'Peasants believe in a fly-like Epidemic Witch Nasav as the personification of infection, which can enter through all openings of the body.' "[2]

---

1 German Fed. Archives, NS19-3103, Page 2
2 German Fed. Archives, NS19-3103, Page 6

The here-mentioned Prof. Dr. Reiner Müller of Cologne University may have stirred up Himmler's interest[1] by his chemical weapons-related work, or by his exposition on race eugenics. And truly, Müller had authored a textbook on hygienics (1935). In the chapter "Soil and Water" is found the subchapter "Waste Products" with another subchapter entitled "Cadavers," and again with another subtitle "Types of Burials." This chapter is subdivided into: "Burial," "Cremation," and "Other types of Burials." In the section "Cremation" is found the following note: "Disadvantages of Cremation … Crematoria fail in the case of mass deaths and on battle fields; e.g. cremations were abandoned for lack of wood in the course of the typhus outbreak in Leningrad in 1921."[2] Under "Other Burials" are found the following methods for the disposal of corpses: Embalmment, Water Burial (on tree trunks or drifting in the Ganges River), Disintegration (in clay vessels in ammonia nitrate) and Air Entombment. The section on Air Entombment refers also to the Parse entombment custom. The Parse originally lived in the area of today's Iran, in Persia, but in the 10th century were driven to India by Muslims. They practice Air Entombment in their "Towers of Silence." Prior to this, Müller briefly mentions Plinius: "Air Entombment. Plinius reports that there were stone coffins called sarcophagi (Meat Eaters); if a corpse were put into one of those, it would have disappeared after 40 days down to the teeth (bones). Since these 'coffins' … stood on posts, carrion flies could enter through cracks, their maggot brood able to consume the soft parts even faster than in 40 days, – Linné already wrote: 'A dead horse will be more quickly consumed by the descendants of three bluebottles than by a lion.' Primitive peoples practice Air Entombment on trees (bird and insect consumption). In Central Asia corpses are laid down openly as food for dogs and wolves [a procedure known to Himmler at the latest since the film report of the Tibet Expedition (where dozens of vultures ate three women) that took place under his patronage.] Also known are the Parse 'Towers of Silence' in Bombay (today's Mumbai): the sacred elements of earth and fire are not to be contaminated by corpses. The corpses disappear in a short time, devoured by vultures; for where there is carrion, 'eagles' gather. Epidemic dispersal was feared, however the danger is minimal".[3] We do not know what concrete cause moved the SS

---

1   I am not aware of any events in the SS-Reichsführer's personal staff that were initiated without Himmler, i.e. his benevolent attention.
2   Müller, Lehrbuch, 126
3   Müller, Lehrbuch, 127. Referring to the erroneous rumors that the corpses of Jewish victims were processed into soap and artificial fertilizer, and to Himmler's order 1942, the "corpses of these deceased Jews," who fell victim to "increase[d] mortality," should

in the midst of war to the inquiry about Nasav. However, one can imagine two scenarios which, for lack of further sources remain speculation: For one, the search for a method of speedy disposal of corpses ("rot"), and second, the search for classical, biological weapons ("infection"). The implication is that in October of 1943, the problem of the necessary disposal of large numbers of corpses was faced. It is then imaginable that a textbook was accessed for assistance wherein this question was specifically addressed. This is likely a textbook on the subject of "Hygiene,' probably by one of the greatest German specialists in this field, Reiner Müller 1943. In his text book the actual protagonists of the decay in air, dogs, wolves, birds of prey, and insects crystallize. Since dogs in our culture are counted among domestic animals, they are ruled out. Wolves are rare, and birds of prey are also not available in the required quantities. Their handling would also be too costly in the still to be built aviaries for corpses. This leaves insects. Larvae can accomplish this task quickly, cost-efficiently and epidemic-free, the larvae of flies. At this point it is obvious to concentrate further investigations on the described custom of Zarathustra-worshippers, the Parse, with special consideration to flies. It is possible that a further publication of Müller's was now taken under advisement, where the above statement about the fly-like Epidemic Witch Nasav was found, or in his "Medical Microbiology" (1 1939), where immediately on page one there is the following statement on the subject: "The Iranians believe in a fly-shaped Epidemic Witch NASAV as the personification of infection, entering the body through all its openings."[1] Since further

---

"either be incinerated or buried," in order to prevent "misuse of the corpses". [see: Himmler, Dienstkalender, 619, footnote 43]

[1] Müller, Mikrobiologie, 1. Unfortunately, its first edition of 1939 was not available to me. It is possible that the first edition contained still the sentence about Nasav, cited by Grawitz, and not the version cited by me dating from 1946. – Perusal of Müller's Mikrobiologie would – had it occurred – have been very much to Himmler's pleasure. The book concludes with a chapter on the subject of "racial hygiene." There, Müller elaborates, among other things: "The term [Racial hygiene] was coined in 1895 by PLOETZ in Munich. As hygiene has as the goal, in the medical sense, the prevention of the pathological and inferior, so racial hygienics wants to prevent pathological and inferior descendants, at first independent of the anthropological races ... Most likely, the word race is not derived, as some have assumed, from the Latin radix, root, or Latin generatio (old French generace), or old German reiza, line, but from the Arabic ras, meaning head, origin. In Spain the word was adopted by the Moors [to this: Wegener, Kelten, 41ff.], and entered German first in the 18th century as the French race. KANT introduced the word in 1775 ('Von den verschiedenen Racen der Menschen') in today's anthropological meaning (E. OBERHUMMER 1928). The term Battle of the Races was

literature on this subject is not accessible due to the war, the investigations of the SS for the promising fly of "decay" (Grawitz), dissolved into nothingness.

The here-described event could have happened in this way and, in the face of the then prevailing circumstances, may be a quite plausible speculation. Meyer's conversational dictionary of 1894 writes in passing about the Beelzebub mentioned by Grawitz: "Beelzebub (Ball-zebub, meaning 'Fly-Baal'), a godhead worshipped by Philistines, especially in Ekron (Sec. of Book of Kings, ch.1, v. 2), a god of oracles. At the time of Christ, Beelzebub appears among Jews in the Gospels as a common term for Satan as the topmost of demons or uncouth spirits."[1] It cannot be excluded that this biblical, Jewish god of flies goes back to the Zoroastic Epidemic Witch Nasav, also seen as a spirit spreading pollution. And truly, there existed diverse adoptions of Zoroastic elements of belief by the spatially proximal Judaism.[2]

The search for alternative solutions in the question for a situation-dependent corpse disposal constitutes a plausible explanation for the, as such, rather bizarre events about the Epidemic Witch Nasav. This is supported especially by the inclusion of the SS Reichsdoctor Grawitz into the events. Had the interest in the Epidemic Witch been more of a religio-philosophic nature, surely the "Ahnenerbe" ("Ancestral Legacy," SS Organisation), but not the Reichsdoctor would have been engaged. It can be assumed that in the fall of 1941, Grawitz was involved in the development of the gas chambers; Zyclon B for the gasification was asked for by the SS-Medical Service under his control.[3] However, besides the question of "decay" acceleration, Müller's reference to Nasav as "personification of infection" could also have triggered the interest of the Reichsführer-SS. To discuss this second possibility to explain the event, a detailed look at the Nasav mythology seems worthwhile:

The knowledge about Nasav originates from the Avesta [literally: the "Text"[4]], the sacred writings of the Parse. As mentioned above, the Parse live nowadays in India near Bombay.[5] At some time in the 10th century they were driven from

---

    introduced especially by GOBINEAU (Essai sur l'inégalité des races humaines 1853)." [Müller, Mikrobiologie, 273]

1  Meyers Konversations-Lexikon, Article "Beelzebub," 5th Edition, 2nd Volume, Leipzig 1894, 672

2  Spiegel, 35 ff. – Pay attention to Satan's incarnation as the swarm of flies in "The Passion of the Christ" by Mel Gibson.

3  Bacharach, Zvi, Article: "Grawitz, Ernst Robert," in: Gutman, 556

4  Spiegel, 45

5  Spiegel, 46

their homes in Persia, today's Iran.[1] They worship the prophet Zarathustra, who, in turn, reverts back to a dualistic realm of gods, suggesting a bright, good god – Ahura Mazda – together with a sinister, evil god – Ahriman.[2] When, at the end of the 18th century, the British language scholar, William Jones,[3] discovered the commonalities of the Indo-Germanic language family, the interest of German philologists became concentrated increasingly on the oriental language area and its traditions. It was obvious now: What could be found there, was simultaneously the heritage of Germanic peoples and, based on its age, probably more authentic[4] than the fragmented transmissions and the later appearance of the north-Germanic mythologies. The language family was named for its geographic area extending between India and the settlement area of the Germanic peoples. Today, it is more appropriately called the "Indo-European" language family since it includes, beside the Germanic languages, also Albanian, Armenian, the Baltic languages, Celtic languages, the Italian (Romance) languages and the Slavic languages. In the search for an Urreligion of this language family, the ancient Persian religion of Zarathustra quickly entered the sight of researchers. However, since Islam was then ruling in Persia, interest quickly focused on the Parse who, in their sacred books preserved the relics of the old Zoroastrian religion with its fire cult. In 1852 F. Spiegel wrote of the Indo-European language family: "Counted among this lineage must be the highly talented civilized peoples of the Old and New World: Indians, Persians, Greeks, Romans, Germanic tribes, Slavs, and maybe the Celts. Every one of these people is a branch of a single Urpeople, whose places of origin have, as of today, not been ascertained, and may possibly never be irrefutably confirmed. It is most likely that in earlier times, these tribes resided together as a single people on the Central Asian plateaus. The emigration of these people from its Urresidence, its separation into individual branches, dates back to before historic times."[5] As an example, Spiegel traces the term God as the Shining-one,[6] back

---

1 Spiegel, 40
2 Spiegel: "Obviously, little is derived from Zarathustra itself in the by us obtained texts of the Avesta, maybe nothing at all; most comes from different and later authors." [Spiegel, 13]
3 For Germany, Franz Bopp, followed suit with "Über das Conjugationssystem der Sanskritsprache," Frankfurt/M. 1816.
4 Spiegel, 59
5 Spiegel, 4
6 Spiegel about the gnostic religion founder Mani who, in the tracks of Zarathustra, revered a god of light: "The Manichaeic religious system is an attempt to found anew religion

to the root div or dyu, to shine: "From it is derived the Sanskrit devas, Latin deus, Lithuanian dievas, Germanic Zio and Tyr, Greek Zeus, and also Jupiter (from Diespiter). The old Persian daêva belongs to the same root . . ."[1] Spiegel 1852 demonstrates the religio-philosophical similarities by referring to a belief in a messiah – found among the Parse and Buddhist beliefs – and, as a replica of these teachings, also with the Jews. Spiegel: "I leave it to others to pursue more completely the similarities of these two views [between Parse and Jewish messiah doctrine]. It may suffice to list here only the main points. According to my opinion, it is the expectation for a worldly, as well as spiritual ruler, which will make his people dominant, regent over its oppressors, but who will also once more unify religion. That the Reich is to last a thousand years is positively articulated everywhere. Just as the Persian view is rather closely related to the Jewish one, one should not overlook that the Buddhist view comes close, too. As is known, developed Buddhism does not suppose a single, but a number of Buddhas, of which one always appears when the teachings of his predecessor have been forgotten. Here, too, it can be demonstrated that the original system is being widened; however, what all northern as well as southern Buddhists expect and agree on is, that the arrival of a new Buddha by the name of Maitreya, which Çâkyamuni himself had proclaimed."[2]

The sacred writings of the Parse are arranged in different subtexts, among which are also found the legal requirements against physical and spiritual impurities, the "Vendidad."[3] These requirements were transmitted to Zarathustra in a dialogue with Ahura Mazda. An example from the first Fargard (chapter) on the

---

    in connection with Parse beliefs, Buddhism, and Christianity. How contemporary this effort was is demonstrated by its wide spread that it soon acquired and the tenaciousness with which it survived the demise of its religious founder to maintain itself far into the Middle Ages ... The narrative of Mani's stay in the cave has likely been copied from the Zarathustra saga, according to which Zarathustra likewise is supposed to have spent several years in such a cave ... Following the presentations we have from Oriental authors, socialistic elements, like the community of women, seem to have formed the main constituent of his doctrine, however, the prohibition for killing animals, let one conclude on a admixture of Buddhist teachings." [Spiegel, 29f.]

1    Spiegel, 6
2    Spiegel, 37. At a different position Spiegel refers in the context of the Persian-Islamic acculturation history to a tale of the Arabian Nights: "These tales depict narratives as to how Parse tortured and imprisoned Muslim youths, then to sacrifice them upon their festivities (compare, e.g. the story of the princess Beder and Kamr essamans), just like similar stories about Jews found with us." [Spiegel, 39]
3    Spiegel, 68. Vendadad literally: the law given against the Daevas. [Spiegel, 287]

creation story: "1. Ahura-mazda spoke to the sacred Zarathustra. 2. I created, oh sacred Zarathustra a place, a creation of grace . . . 6. The Airyana-vaêja of good creation. [Spiegel: These lands must likely be placed into the extreme east of the Iranian Plateau."] 7. Then, an opposition of his created Agra-mainyus, who is full of death. 8. A great snake and winter, the [evil] Daevas[1] created. 9. There, ten are winter months, two are summer months. 10. And those are cold on water, cold on earth, cold on trees."[2]

Then, in the third chapter of the Vendidad, one finds mentioned for the first time the Fly-like Epidemic Witch Nasav, which here, in the original, is called Drukhs Naçus.[3] Ahura Mazda explains to Zarathustra on the subject of entombment cult: "44. Any single one must not carry a dead. 45. If a single one carries it, the dead: 46. Then the Naçus contaminates through the nose, from the eye, from the tongue, from the face, from the anus. 47. Onto those (meaning those committing this sin) nails leaps the Drukhs Naçus."[4] Following Parse teachings, the dead body is unclean, and there is danger that it will also contaminate its surroundings. Thus, it is not to be buried so as not to contaminate the sacred element of earth, and may also not be incinerated, since it then pollutes the sacred fire of the Parse. Therefore, the Air Entombment, for – as per Ahura Mazda: "No corpse, carried off by dogs, birds, wolves, wind or flies dirties a human being."[5] Nasav is the demonic personification of contamination. Thus, asks Zarathustra, what happens if a man dies in a room where many people are present: "83. Creator! When men are together in the same house, on the same resting place or the same mat . . . 86. One of these men dies on – on how many of these men will the Drukhs Naçus come to rest with decomposition, rot and dirt. 87. To this Ahura-mazda replied: If it is a priest, Drukhs Naçus will leap to, oh sacred Zarathustra."[6] Upon the question when does the Drukhs

---

1   Spiegel: "It may be a coincidence that Ahura, the highest god of the Persians, is expelled to the evil spirits as Asura by the later Indians, which is why one can hardly see him as such, when the devas of the Indians have become the daêvas with Persians as the evil spirits and helpers of the Agra-mainys, when Indra, the highest god of early Hinduism, is, as Andra, also in hell, when Çarva appears also as an evil spirit ... One may assume that religious reasons have been the partial reason for the separation."
2   Spiegel, 61 f.
3   Müller could refer in his books concerning the Nasav to Cyril Elgood's publications to the Persian medical history. – "Drukhs Naçus" is in English frequently represented as "Druj Masu."
4   Spiegel, 82
5   Spiegel, 104
6   Spiegel, 109

Naçus appear? the response is: "Right after death, oh sacred Zarathustra, life's consciousness escapes. 4. This Drukhs Naçus leaps in from the northern areas in the shape of a fly, with evil attack, screaming, and boundless dismemberment of the worst Khrafçtras."[1] At the Towers of Silence, the Dakhmas, on which the dead are laid out, offered to birds of prey as food, the evil spirits will gather: "140. Similarly, oh sacred Zarathustra, the Daevas will gather at these Dakhmas to copulate. 141. As you, being human, in this with bodies-gifted world eat cooked food and cooked meat. 142. Therefore, listen you people and consider that you eat. 143. For this is the pleasure of the Daevas. 144. Everything to which stink adheres. 145. For in these Dakhmas is gathered decomposition, illness, hot fever, uncleanness, cold fever, trembling and old hair. 146. In these Dakhmas, people are the most deadly."[2] The Daevas created the Naçus as the lowest of demons. Thus spoke Zarathustra: "I will beat the creation, produced by the Daevas; I will beat the Naçus, the Daevas have created."[3] How can a path be cleaned on which dead have been carried? Ahura Mazda: "41. By leading a yellowish dog with four eyes [probably meaning: Eyes plus skin spots above the lids] or a white one with yellow ears across. 44. This causes the Drukhs Naçus to flee to the northern areas [from which it came]." Spiegel: "This custom, of employing dogs as cleaning entities at funeral ceremonies surely hides an ancient Indo-Germanic idea."[4] Another means of expelling the Nasav, are invocation slogans spoken by a priest: "62. I drive off the Drukhs, run away oh Drukhs! I drive off the Drukhs, for it to tumble toward the north, not must it kill the body-engifted world of the pure."[5] If this exorcism is not properly performed, there is the danger of strengthening the Nasav: "This Drukhs Naçus will then be more deadly than before. 176. It increases illnesses, death and oppositions like before." As a punishment, the non-authorized exorcist is to be beheaded.[6]

To summarize: The Nasav is subordinate to the Daevas, a lower, fly-shaped demon, living in Persia's north. Upon a death, the Nasav comes quickly, without being called. However, it can be beseeched, even exorcised, meaning, it can be addressed. A wrong address makes it even more "deadly," meaning that it not only appears as an agent of decomposition after death, but can also cause death

---

1 Spiegel, 124. Spiegel points out that A. Kuhn had proved by the form "druh" the "Drukhs Naçus" also in the Indian Vedas. [Spiegel, 124]
2 Spiegel, 134 f.
3 Spiegel, 244
4 Spiegel, 142 f.
5 Spiegel, 144
6 Spiegel, 172

to spread from the dead to the living. This makes it the agent of infection, or as Müller writes, according to the SS Reichsdoctor, the "personification of infection." One can imagine that the Nasav did not just simply appear to the SS as an agent of "decomposition," but truly as an agent of "infection," deserving investigation. The bacteriologist, Müller, cited by Grawitz, was not only a hygienist but also an expert in chemical and biological weapons: In his speech delivered on January 18, 1933, at the Reichs-inaugural celebration of the Cologne University he expressed himself extensively about "Germany's Defense against chemical and bacteriological attacks." The historical excursus about the employment of poison gas in World War I was followed by a discussion of required preventive measures for the protection of soldiers and the civilian population in a future war, ending with an entreaty on the threatening danger from the East. In the historical part of his speech, Müller elaborated: ... well before the Haag Agreement that chemical weapons were employed. Homer's sulphur-dioxide by which Odysseus smoked out the dining room of his Penelope after the slaying of her suitors, 'with fire and curse-averting sulphur.' This method was, as Thukydides reports, decisively applied by the Peloponesians 2,257 years ago upon the siege of Delion. The $SO_2$ forced the Delians to surrender. – As reported by Jul. Meyer, about 1577, the Austrian Veit Wulff recommended the use of arsenic smoke balls (poison gas) for the conquest of forts; but it would be such an awful thing, that Christians should not employ it against Christians, but solely against Turks and other infidels.[!]"[1] About World War I, Müller writes: "Health conditions on the western front were rather satisfactory concerning epidemics, except for the first half year. At times, one would hear mockingly that hygiene was to blame for the war taking so long. Certainly, 50 years earlier, such trench warfare would have become an epidemic catastrophe. However, when an epidemic arose against which we, even today, know no applicable protection, going by the name of 'Spanish Illness', the Influenza vera, it spread within a few days, with prisoners coughing and sneezing, and droplets moved across barbed wire and trenches."[2] Müller brooded about Europe's future: "The white race must reckon that, a few decades from now, a mighty, even greater empire may arise, whose population increase will not, as in earlier times, be inhibited by epidemics ... As yet, the leading position of the predominant Germanic peoples can still be saved ... But without a viable Germany, Europe's fate is endangered."[3] Here, Müller, as

---

1     Müller, Abwehr, 7
2     Müller, Abwehr, 22
3     Müller, Abwehr, 26

an aside, suggests two things: 1. The First World War was not only ended by troops, but also by epidemics, among which was the Spanish Flue. 2. In the past, the population increases of eastern peoples were strongly kept in check, so that the Germanic peoples were not threatened by them. Müller's sketched historic examples of the employment of poison gas. For instance, the use of arsenic in the fight against Turks and other infidels, seems to make sense to conduct an investigation of the medical history of similar events. The deathly effects of infection following exposure to the Nasav might describe such a process. This would also help to explain the effort for further investigations, which, with reference to a mere decomposition-accelerated objective by fly maggots does not seem to be compelling: This process is also well known in Europe and does not require an historic development. Moreover, the outlook is enticing: An epidemic, against which one's own population can be inoculated in time, would make it possible to depopulate large areas in the East rather discretely. By this means, one could create space for the colonists "Space in the East." To explain the process, both variants – the disposal of corpses and bacteriological weapons development – are plausible, but in the light of poor sources, remain speculative.

Sisters Kate and Margaret Fox, who, in the middle of the 19th century, triggered the "Big Bang" of modern spiritualism, when they claimed to hear the knocking noises of ghosts. (Webb, Underground, 194)

# 5 The Spirits: Du Prel, Jürgens, Fidler, zur Bonsen, Heise

The big bang of modern spiritualism happened in 1847: Maggie and Katharina Fox, in Hydesville, New York State, suddenly heard a mysterious knocking. Did the spirit of a deceased want to tell them something? No, it did not. Subsequently, the sisters admitted to have produced the "Hydesville Knocking" themselves. Now, they were no longer believed. The events overran their creators.[1] The news of the mysterious ghostly knocking quickly reached Europe. Seemingly confirmed by ever new discoveries in physics which disclosed a before unforeseen spectrum of until then unknown radiations – Röntgen radiation (1895), electromagnetic waves (Hertz 1883), radioactive radiation (Becquerel 1886), or the wireless (1900)[2] – now gripped Europe in a wave of spiritualism. Early on, the Swedish scholar, Emanuel Swedenborg (1688-1772), had an important influence on the German occult scene. Johannes Heinrich Jung-Stilling, especially, edited his work for the German-speaking area in his "Theory of Spirit Knowledge" which appeared in 1808. Alfred Lehmann wrote of him: "Jung-Stilling's theory is notable for the reason that it almost anticipates modern occultism. Man consists of body, soul or nerve spirit, and spirit. The spirit is of divine origin. Its observational power would be unlimited, if it were not tied to the body by the nerve spirit. Mesmer-treatment can largely remove this connection between body and spirit, freeing the observational powers of the somnambulists (sleep walkers); they become spatially and temporally clairvoyant, and may even get as far as seeing ghosts."[3] Besides Swedenborg, Jung-Stilling went back to Franz Anton Mesmer (1734-1815), a doctor of the 18th century. Mesmer believed to be able to cure by influencing a supposed physical Fluidum in the body of his patients by means of magnets. Later, magnets were given up, and touch by a *magnetizer* had to suffice. As a consequence, the pa-

---

1   Stutterheim: "As adults (1887/88), Maggie and Katharina Fox gave public lectures wherein they explained how they had produced the knocking noises ... Their explanations were not believed, rather the knocking ghosts were believed." [Stutterheim, 55] Webb: "Finally, in 1888, Maggie snapped and confessed. She gave 'séances' before a large audience and demonstrated how the [table-] knocking had been produced." [Webb, Underground, 18]
2   Stutterheim, 71
3   Lehmann, Alfred: Aberglaube und Zauberei von den ältesten Zeiten an bis in die Gegenwart, Stuttgart 1898, 293, here citing Stutterheim, 53

Precursor of spiritualism: Johannes Jung-Stilling, in his "Geisterkunde (Ghost Knowledge)" (1808) fell back on Emanuel Swedenborg (1688-1772) and Anton Mesmer (1734-1815).

tient frequently fell into magnetic sleep, which, the opposite of sleep walking was called "artificial" somnambulism – today, we speak of hypnosis which, as ever, enjoys great popularity with psychotherapy. Later, Romantic Natural Philosophy willingly picked up on Mesmer's ideas and that of his students, with Fluidum, somnambulism and Lucidity (clairvoyance) magnificently fitting into the concept of Romantic Natural Philosophy. Following this idea, the cosmos is a living organism pervaded by a soul holding the entirety as well as its parts together. Accordingly, the magnetic Fluidum would have then been such a force: could it have been proved, it would have confirmed the Romantic concept.[1]

The wave of spiritualism caught also Scandinavia. By the end of the 19th century, it was reported from Sweden that a dead person had reappeared and had transmitted a message to his dependent. The materialization of the Swede was photographed with the photo presented to old acquaintances and relatives. With that it seemed that finally proof of the existence of the spirit realm had been provided. Written by Matthias Fidler, the story entitled, "The Dead live," was translated into German by Fritz Feilgenhauer with the "encouragement of

---

[1] see Groth, Peter: "Die Stigmatisierte Nonne Anna Katharina Emmerick – Eine Krankengeschichte im Zeitalter der Romantik – zwischen preußischer Staatsraison und katholischer Erneuerung," 1996, pdf under http://www.in-output.de/AKE/

the secretary of the scientific association 'Sphinx'[1], Mr. Max Rahn, Berlin."[2] For the translator, it was important, as he wrote 1895 in the foreword, to present the unambiguous "Proof of Identity of the Deceased," for the "survival of deceased human spirits."[3] Thus, his interests tallied with those of the author's book, who wrote: "My intention is only to present that at least *one* person of our time, the 19th century, truly lived and died, yet, after his death, according to my opinion, brought proof of his continued existence." According to Fidler, all this began on April 3, 1890, when a girlfriend of his presented to him in his office in Gothenburg various business letters and also, unexpectedly, a note with the lettering "Sven Strömberg." In the presence of friends, the girlfriend's hand later wrote more messages, like: "Strömberg wants you to tell his folks that he's dead; he died on the thirteenth of March, in Wisconsin, I think, he says."[4] In later sessions, the spirit even materialized: "I fully and clearly saw now the head and shoulders of a man standing behind the lady in the small room;

---

[1] Between January 1885 to June 1896 the monthly publication "Sphinx – Monatsschrift für die geschichtliche und experimentale Begründung der übersinnlichen Weltanschauung auf monistischer Grundlage" ["Sphinx for the historic and experimental justification of extrasensory world view on a monistic basis,"] was published by Dr. jur. Wilhelm Hübbe-Schleiden [Chairman of the German Theosophical Society in Elberfeld]. Kerstin Stutterheim evaluated the magazine as follows: "This between 1886 and 1895 published magazine was of great importance for the revival of occultism in Germany." [Stutterheim, 61] Goodrick-Clarke elaborated: "Max Dessoir wrote explanatory articles on hypnosis, Eduard von Hartmann created a philosophy of 'individualism,' which, before the background of Kant's theories, Christian doctrine and spiritualistic speculation claimed, that the 'Self' survived death as a disembodied unit. Carl du Prel, the psychologist, and his colleague, Lazar von Hellenbach, who had conducted séances with the famous American medium Henry Slade in Vienna, wrote treatises in a similar vein. Another important member of the Sphinx-Circle was Karl Kiesewetter, whose studies of the history of esoteric tradition after the Renaissance had made knowledge about the learned magicians, modern alchemists, and contemporary occultism accessible to a broad public." [Goodrick-Clarke, Nicholas: Die okkulten Wurzeln des Nationalsozialismus, Graz/Stuttgart 1997, 28; here citing Stutterheim, 61] The directory of the entire 124 issues with their 3070 article titles are presently found on the Internet under: http://www.austheos.org.au/indices/SPHINXHU.HTM. Among others publishing there: Friedrich Eckstein, Albert von Schrenck-Notzing [Freiherr, Psychoanalyst, Legal Counsel, 1862-1929 [Stutterheim, 74, 77]], Gustav Theodor Fechner [the gnostic advocated the hypothesis that the planets were themselves animated, with plants likewise]

[2] Fidler, 4

[3] Fidler, 4 f.

[4] Fidler, 9 f.

not I alone, but all the others present saw the male figure as well as the lady's."¹ For his investigations into the deceased's past, Fidler wrote to a consul in Winnipeg, Canada, sending him a photo of the materialization with the question: "Is there some similarity between the picture sent by me and his [still present] portrait]?" His reply was: "A great one; however, an even greater one is with his still living brother. The dead wore no beard."² From this and other evidence, the author concluded: "From this, one can draw the natural conclusion that, when *one* person continues to live after death, also *all others continue to do so* ... I, for my part, admit without doubt that the acting force emanates from human spirits who lived here on Earth, as we live, and, therefore, the time will come, when we, too, will pass through this same change ... after the great transition through the so-called pearly gates of death."³ Heinrich Himmler must have been strongly moved by this content: He twice read the book in 1921. His comment: "Much speaks for the book's content being true. However, against it one can see especially the similarity of the photography with the brother of the deceased. But I rather believe the material to be flawless. If this is the case, important new foundations have been laid. – Transmigration of souls."⁴

Based on the background of the reports coming from the USA about ghostlike happenings, the Munich philosopher⁵ Freiherr Dr. phil. Carl du Prel developed his work. He became the mentor of German spiritualism research in the 19th century. Du Prel attempted to unite Darwinism with spiritualism, departing from the consideration that Nature, in the course of evolution, and under the very different physical laws of other worlds, had also created also other organs and other capabilities: "No reasonable person will insist that the millions of inhabited⁶ stars are only here to endlessly repeat the organic problem of the retina and the eustachian trumpet."⁷ It was his goal to produce scientifically irrefutable proof of the existence of a ghostly realm beyond our reality. To confirm this parallel world, he traveled through Europe, took part in séances, investigated eerie events and, in principle, pursued that which today is comprised by the term parapsychology. Heinrich Himmler read his Reclam-booklet, entitled "Spiritualism," in January/February of 1923. – In November 1923, the 23 year-

---

1  Fidler, 13
2  Fidler, 30
3  Fidler, 35 f.
4  Himmler, Leseliste, Subject entry No. 86
5  Prel, 76
6  See also: Prel, Carl du: Die Planetenbewohner, Leipzig 1880 [Prel, 8]
7  Prel, 16

old Himmler participated in the Putsch at the Munich Feldherrnhalle. The first edition of the publication had already appeared in Leipzig in 1893.

As a case history, du Prel cited a medium in Milano, Eusapia Paladino, who, in 1892, supposedly convinced the well-known professor [Cesare] Lombroso and some of his colleagues.[1] He described the medium: "Eusapia is a rather small, but well-proportioned, lively Italian about 35 years of age, though without any schooling. She is married but childless, however, it should be mentioned that she has adopted two orphans. In her normal condition she speaks in her Neapolitan dialect, but pure Italian when she is in a trance."[2] Du Prel participated in six sessions with her. By way of Eusapia, "John" revealed himself as the controlling spirit. He is said to have communicated with those present by means of tapping signals heard from inside the table. But it also happened differently: "Often John spoke through the medium to us and that in her normal condition, at which – as it appeared to us – he employed the means of suggestion, but often also by putting her into a trance – recognizable by the upturned pupils – and from which she spoke in that chaste way already described by old Psellus ... We used a substantial part of our time, and those in lighted sessions, on ascertaining table movements and rises without mechanical influence ... Such horizontal table rises were on average 30 to 40 cm high, and lasted for about a second, sufficient time for taking a photograph. Afterwards, the table dropped noisily down onto all four feet simultaneously."[3] Also present was the astronomer Prof. Schiaparelli, Director of the *Occervatorio di Bera*, the "researcher who discovered the straight lines or canals on planet Mars."[4] He stated that he had even felt with his hands the materialization of a being in the room: "One of the experimenters, Schiaparelli, could vouch, only to a certain degree, the materialization of a head. This was because of the darkness, and because he was able to conclude only from his sense of touch, the head shape and hair, which he thought felt about 30 cm above the table." When du Prel had put his hand behind a curtain, it was supposedly shaken by a ghost: "... when I, with a 'Good Night, John!' pushed my hand through a gap in the curtain, it was vehemently

---

1   Alexander Aksakow (imperial Russian Council of State of St. Petersburg [Prel, 76] and the "Psychic Studies" published by him, had, as stated by du Prel, introduced spiritualism to Germany. He refers to his article "Animismus und Spiritismus," Leipzig 1890. [Prel, 73f.]
2   Prel, 77
3   Prel, 78 ff.
4   Prel, 76

shaken, and the same happened when several other gentlemen did the same."[1] In the face of this clear body of evidence du Prel arrived at the conclusion: "With the finding of the conformity of spiritualistic phenomena, no other conclusion can naturally be reached than that all the world will believe in spiritualism in the coming century."[2]

In the theoretical part of his book – chapter "The Phenomenology of Spiritualism" – du Prel differentiated between animism and spiritualism. On animism, he summarized all those phenomena where a living soul (*anima*) was standing next to itself in order to even materialize, that is to say, become visible, whereas in spiritualism the soul of a non-living played the leading role. It, too, could materialize. Thus, in animism a medium' soul could appear during a séance in the room. In this case, the medium would not be the cause but the requirement for the appearance of an "invisible or only an exceptionally visible intelligent being,"[3] at which time du Prel spoke of spiritualism. Du Prel granted the soul to have preexistence and post-existence. "This soul is not equivalent with consciousness, but lies outside our consciousness; it is the original element of our individuality, but not, say, only a psychic element, but a power center, which thinks as well as organizes ... an organized soul [see the Entelechy of Aristotle] must survive death and, in so doing, obviously preserves its organizing capability, of which it makes use at materializations ..."[4] Proof for such materializations were provided by photographic plates [precursors of Negatives], which proved that it could not be hallucinations.[5] Also, the phenomena could not be explained by referring to the subconscious. Only the existence of a transcendental subject [likely acc. to his teacher Lazar Baron Hellenbach von Paczoloy, 1827-1887[6]] would be suited to explain the events.[7] The consciousness was said to be an enemy of this subject; it must step back in favor of the transcendental: "This is why we see it almost as a general rule that the mystical activity and passivity is the prerequi-

---

1  Prel, 82 f.
2  Prel, 97
3  Prel, 35
4  Prel, 36
5  Prel, 37. Du Prel did not see Kant's "Träume eines Geistersehers" as a critique, but as Kant's agreement with spiritualism: "Kant, too, was of the opinion, and spoke of them in 'Träume eines Geistersehers,' in that we simultaneously belong to this life as well as to the beyond, without being aware of it as earthly people." [Prel, 19]
6  Example of title: Hellenbach, Lazar Baron von: "Geburt und Tod als Wechsel der Anschauungsform oder die Doppel-Natur des Menschen", Leipzig 1885
7  Prel, 52

site for the suppression of sensory consciousness. The same is true in magnetic somnambulism and the trance of media."[1] The psychological subconscious was to have its starting point in the brain's activities, which served as the source and venue of the presentations, not so, however, for the transcendental unconscious. Here, the brain was thought to be solely a passive receiver. Du Prel: "But with the insane, it showed, however, what is unknown to our psychiatrists, which, by itself suffices, Hartmann [Eduard von Hartmann, critic of spiritualism[2]] to disprove that this being's consciousness is intact as soon as they are put into magnetic somnambulism."[3] It is the opinion of spiritualists regarding the question of "spiritualistic immortality" that the "phenomena at the base of the soul survive death,"[4] This belief lead to a "transcendental optimism," said to conflict with earthly pessimism. One of the reasons for the optimistic outlook to the future, happy condition: sleepwalkers feel happy while they walk. The experience of the mystics would also speak for it: "This is why the Christian mystics explained the ecstatic conditions as 'rapture into heaven.' Finally, this is why the Indian mystic sees in ecstasy the merging with Brahma, i.e. becoming God."[5] The echo of gnostic motives cannot be missed. Himmler commented on his reading experience with the words: "A small scientific work, with a philosophical basis, really let me believe in spiritualism and was the first to truly introduce me to it."[6] The doubts Himmler had with respect to the deceased Swede, had been dispersed. Now, two years later, he believed in spiritualism.

Himmler's interest in the subject area of spiritualism did not remain limited to theory. In 1925, he read a practical guide to pendulum use by Heinrich Jürgens.[7] The practical guide, "Practice and Magic of Pendulum use," was understood as "Instruction for the use of the sideric[8] pendulum for the purpose

---

1 Prel, 62 f.
2 Hartmann, Eduard von: "Der Spiritsmus", Leipzig 1885. To which Aksakow reacted with "Animismus und Spiritismus." [Prel, 26]
3 Prel, 66
4 Prel, 67
5 Prel, 68
6 Himmler, Leseliste, Title 148
7 Himmler, Reading list, Title 246, Transcript page 37
8 Jürgens explains the "sideric pendulum movement" as: "literally star-like, meaning acting through [odic] radiation" [Jürgens, 8] Stutterheim: "Paracelsus [Renaissance-Alchemist, believed that the cosmos consisted on a higher plane of a trinity of quicksilver, sulfur, and salt; born Theophrast Bombast von Hohenheim 1493, died 1541] assumed that the body consisted of two different material parts: of a 'sideric part' and an 'elementary part' of earth and water. Building on it, he explained spook phenomena as the 'walk' and the

of diagnosing illnesses and human character features, sex determination, and questioning of otherworldly persons".[1] In view of his presented creed on the subject of spiritualism in 1923, it is very probable that Himmler was less interested in sex, character, or illness definitions, but rather in, as promised by the subtitle of the book, the "questioning of the otherworldly" – in establishing a contact between the spirit and ghost realm, a conversation with the dead. The book provides templates with imprinted letter and numeric fields and pendulum terms like "no, yes, left, right, evil, good, alive, dead ..."[2] In addition, the book's buyer could immediately order from the publisher for "1 mark - free postage and handling" the required horseshoe pendulum "Method Jürgens."[3] For others, practical do-it-yourself instructions were available.[4]

The pendulum's function was justified in the author's instructions with the effect of a secretive force, the force of the "Od." Similarly, as in matters of Mesmerism, it addressed the question of the transition from sprit to matter, from body to soul. Although it had, in the meantime, been established that weak currents caused even the muscles of dead animals to contract, it assisted in the spiritual will's conversion into physical action, but more complex controls did not seem possible. In 1844, the chemist Freiherr Dr. Karl Ludwig von Reichenbach[5] (1788-1869) opined that he had discovered a new power, a new medium, the "Od." Reichenbach gave a good example for the close connection of trial and error between the natural sciences and spiritualism, for, as a chemist and industrialist, he had invented paraffin and the antiseptic creosote. Thus, he stood on both legs in life. However, this did not prevent him from turning at

---

    perception of the sideric part, which had separated itself from the elementary part of a deceased who had died from a strong affect. This idea appears again in the theosophical concept of 'aetheric double' and the 'astral body'." [Stutterheim, 47f.]

1    Jürgens, Title
2    Jürgens, 26
3    Jürgens, 7
4    Jürgens, 7
5    Examples of his titles: Reichenbach, Karl: "Untersuchungen über den Magnetismus und damit verwandte Gegenstände," Heidelberg 1845; "Physikalisch-physiologische Untersuchungen über die Dynamide des Magnetismus, der Elektrizität, der Wärme, des Lichts, der Krystalisation, des Chemismus, in ihren Beziehungen zur Lebenskraft", 2nd printing, Braunschweig 1850; "Der sensitive Mensch und sein Verhalten zum Ode," Stuttgart 1854, "Odisch-magnetische Briefe," Stuttgart 1856; "Die Pflanzenwelt in ihrer Beziehung zur Sensitivität und zum Ode", Vienna 1858; *Les effluves odiques: conférences faites en 1866 par le baron Reichenbach à l'Académie I. et R. des Sciences de Vienne*, Paris 1897

the beginning of 1841, to the investigation of the Od. Assumably, Reichenbach drew the designation "Od" from the nordic god Odin. Its power differs from the Mesmeric Fluidum by the claim that it is of dual polarity. The author of "Pendulum Practice" cited an epigone of Reichenbach's with the words: "We know electricity and can therefore determine whether there are places in the tissue of an organism where sufficient quantities of this energy type can form, whether there are systems which, with a distant analogy to motors, can convert this energy into a mechanical one, and whether finally the so-called motoric nerves, i.e. those that control the movement impulses to muscles emanating from the brain are conduits for the electrical current. *We do not find anything of this sort in the organism* ... The kind and speed of impulse conduct in motoric nerves exists without any analogy in the study of electrics. Chemical analogies also ... fail completely ... [we know today that the conduct of impulses is very clearly transmitted in an electo-chemical way]. We can therefore not claim with certainty that the organism works *with a specific*, by the official physics still not recognized method. This force of nature, according to the author's conviction, is *the Od. It is recognizable to people with a particular, increased perceptive faculty, Reichenbach calls Sensitivity, recognizable by touch and eyes. Od is continuously transmitted by the human body*, primarily through *the fingertips* and the head's openings, the eyes, the ears, and the mouth. The radiations of the right hand are perceived in a dark room by some Sensitives as a blue light, those of the left as a red light. Reichenbach assumes polarity of the Od in the organism as well as the globe ..." Jürgens: "The French researcher Durville determined that magnetism also manifested itself as a source of the Od, or its radiation, respectively. The Vienna doctor Dr. Friedrich Feerhow [this is Friedrich Wehofer, who, at the beginning of the 20th century publicized diverse Reichenbach reprints[1]], said that all nerves of the human body were conduits of the Od and that simultaneously these nerves were odistic self-illuminators ... [Dr. Fritz] Quade proposes in his 'Odik' the working hypothesis that the Od could consist of *Uratoms*, claiming that the Uratoms would be polar like the Od and found in all known chemical matter."

Then, Jürgens cites Feerhow, who picks up the classical concept of the *Blickstrahl*, the looking beam, when he writes: "Looking also exerts odic influence in that, by its effect, the looked-at person is odically irradiated. The human Od-Light is substantially stronger than that of all shining magnets and crystals

---

[1] One of Feerhow's own titles: Feerhow, Friedrich: N-Strahlen und Od: ein Beitrag zum Problem der Radioaktivität des Menschen, Leipzig 1912

... In darkness the human body is seen *shining in its entirety* by Sensitive. It is enveloped in a shining, odic atmosphere that seems to enlarge it, giving it the appearance of a white, ghostlike monster."[1]

Without difficulty, one recognizes in the expositions of the Od-theoreticians the gnostic, metaphysical light,[2] here merely scientifically veiled. In 1922, it was said of it by the Munich Alfred Schuler, an occultist from the incubation phase of National Socialism: "Imagine a vibrating light complex which, in reciprocal friction, consisting of innumerable active and passive lit up electrons / a Fluidum in restless movement / is the substance of the universe. These Fluide are the nimbus [a kind of halo][3] / the aureole-creating force / which encloses us / all entities ..."[4] The gnostic dimension of the Od-beginnings becomes, at the latest, unmistakable with Jürgens' closing words: "Once God's spirit has awoken in us, it will become possible for us to draw the consequences and to bring our higher Self in continuous contact with the all-infusing cosmic force, without which there is and will be nothing. This will lead us from the unconscious sphere to the conscious sight of higher spiritual worlds, turning us into shining human beings, taking us to an über-consciousness, and into the *land of the shining*!"[5] God is already in man; he must only awaken, the "Higher Self" – the spark of the soul of divine central light sunk into the realm of matter – must only find again the connection with the all-infusing force, from the unconscious sphere (the sleep of the as yet not recognizing human). He must find his way to the conscious. This means that by insight, through the gnosis-awakened sighting of the über-consciousness, the all-connecting, divine source of radiation, he will finally re-enter the *pleroma,* the fullness of light, the "land of the shining." According to his massage therapist, Kersten, Himmler remarked in 1942: "We only go so far as to say that racially pure, Germanic blood, is the precondition for the highest spiritual and mental characteristics and will be delighted should this idea ever find greater acceptance. However, this covers only the purely bio-

---

1   Jürgens, 6
2   Details with: Wegener, Schuler, 39
3   Klages: "The ancients knew the genius loci, the nimbus, the aura, and we also speak still of the 'Atmosphere' of a person, an house, an area. This 'Atmosphere,' perceived by so-called sensitive natures, perceived by sensitive, unknown to more robust minds, is a reality." [cited here, following Pauen, Michael, article: Wahlverwandtschaft wider Willen? – Rezeptionsgeschichte und Modernität von Ludwig Klages, in: Großheim, Perspektiven, 21]
4   Müller, Augen, 220 ff.
5   Jürgens, 29

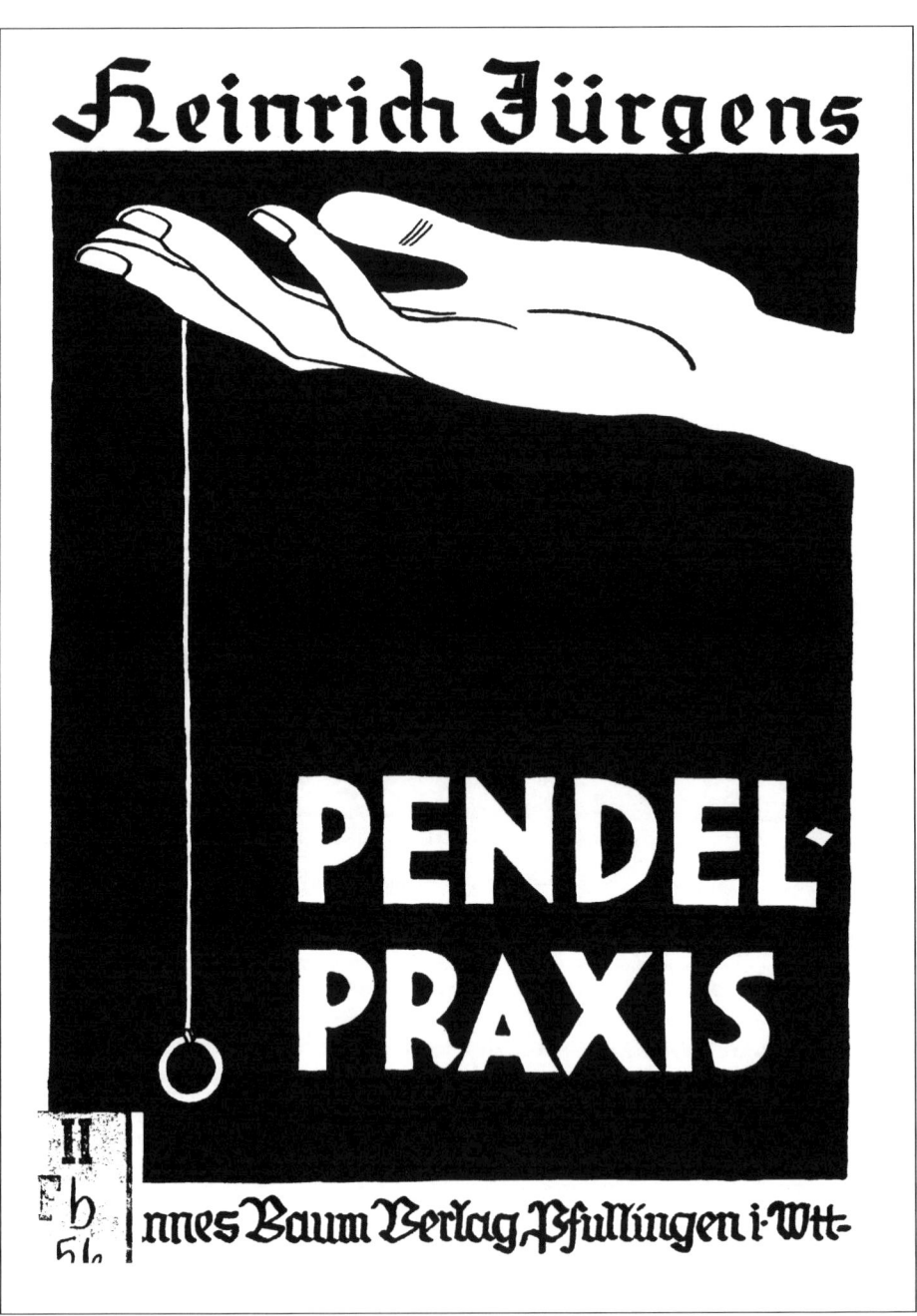

„Pendelpraxis" read by Himmler in 1925

logical part of the problem. Purebred blood is, however, also the precondition for bright forces and essences, kindred to us and materialized in our Germanic people. Here lies the religious side of the problem."[1]

To the question of how the Od enters the body, the author of pendulum practice that appeared in 1925, also has an answer: "The two most important sources of the Od in the organism are *the flame-less conversion* of nutrients in the lungs and tissues and the intake of the Od by breathing. The more nutrients that are combusted, the more Od is developed. It is entirely probable that the precise conversion at 37 degrees or even lower temperatures will create relatively *more Uratoms*, i.e. *etheric matter* and fewer electrons. Not all people are able to take the same quantity of Od from the air. What the Indians call 'Prana' (the life force of the 'German Yoga School') seems to be the Od."

Here, Jürgens equates Od with the legendary Ether, already mentioned by Aristotle, next to fire, air, earth and water the fifth essence, the *quinta essentia*. Kerstin Stutterheim, seeing only the physical definition, elaborates about the ether: "The Ether or Light-ether was invented in the 19th century as filling the universe with something wherein the light waves, radiating warmth, magnetism, or gravity could continue to manifest themselves. The ideas about *ether* and *light-ether* also tied in with the theory of a *fourth dimension*. Of major importance to occult theories about ether was the book, published in 1876. '*The Unseen Universe*' by the Britons Balfour Stewart and Peter Guthrie Tait. They described the existence of an 'invisible universe, beyond the *small circle of light* that we call the universe of scientific perception.' '*The Unseen Universe*' also impressed Helena Blavatsky very much. In her first book, 'The unveiled Isis,' she addressed the published thesis of the ether of Tait/Stewart's as cosmic energy storage, using it for her own theory. The 'ether or astral light' also records visual impressions, or 'Daguerreotypes, of all our activities,' and beyond that records images in a 'great image gallery.' Such galleries 'are now hidden at distant and inaccessible locations: the Himalayas in Tibet, subterranean India, and in other secret areas'."[2]

What practical use can be drawn from knowledge about the Od, i.e. the ether? Jürgens concludes with Quade: "When, e.g. a Yoga student succeeds ... in guiding his breath in a specific way through the lungs ... and he directs his

---

1  Kersten, 193. Himmlers enthusiasm for Islam was, however, rationally contingent on defense technology. According to Kersten, Himmler remarked: "Muhammad knew that most people are miserable cowards and are stupid. This is why he promised every warrior who fought bravely in battle and died, two beautiful women as reward ... nothing is so primitive that it isn't believed." [Kersten, 203-205]
2  Stutterheim, 71 f.

spiritual will onto the plentiful inhalation of this fine, etheric matter, he gains powers which enable him to subsist for a long time without food. Man ... is able to accomplish extraordinary feats with respect to muscle activity, as well as mental power."[1] In this way it is possible to achieve through control of the Od, i.e. the ether, a supreme goal, which Jürgens, in his introduction, formulates: "Magic! ... Magic is the soul's, the spirit's power! Conscious control of fine and course matter."[2]

The ether was integrated by Schuler in his most important lecture series "The Nature of the eternal City": "With my eye turned inward I see a vibrating fullness of light, uncounted, in the enjoyment of change-flashing Fluides, the eternally uninterrupted *Wedding in the Ether*."[3] Much has been speculated about whether and to what extent Hitler paid attention to Schuler's theories. In view of Himmler's reading the "Pendulum Practice," it may be said here: The Reichsführer-SS became, at a later period, very familiar with the natural science-garnished new edition of a radiating Fluiden from Od and ether secularized Pleroma[4] after reading "Pendulum Practice" in 1925.

In his Himmler monograph, Ackermann referred in 1970 to Achim Besgen, who, by referencing Felix Kersten, Himmler's massage therapist, wrote: Himmler "was firmly convinced that one could invoke ghosts and enter into regular contact with them. However, as he, at times, granted Kersten, one would have to have a certain talent for it. He suggested that one could only call up ghosts of those deceased for more than a hundred years ... While dozing, the ghost of King Henry often appeared to him to give him valuable advice ... Before important decisions, Himmler had his two astrologers come to present him with his horoscope ... Himmler often emphasized that the astrologers were of the unanimous opinion that Germany could only rise and heal once all Jews had been exterminated ..."[5]

---

1    Jürgens, 4-6
2    Jürgens, 3
3    Klages, Fragmente, 160
4    Pleroma: Gnostic term for Abundance of Light
5    Kersten 1953: "I know, for instance, that Himmler is very superstitious; he believes in good and evil spirits. Although he does not want to admit it, he occupies himself with astrology and at times, has himself advised by at least two astrologers in order to weigh their statements, even if he maintains a certain skepticism." [Kersten, 183] Kersten: "I have discussed this latter question at length with Brandt, who explained to me that he knew precisely that the Reichsführer considered himself as a reincarnation of Henry the Lion. He supposedly was familiar with this story like no one else and considered his eastern settlement as a major event of Germanic history." [Kersten, 190] When, at least,

It was not only dialogue with the dead, like with King Henry I, which fasci-

the statements about Himmler's conversations with the dead Henry I fit the picture well (Himmler was, in any case, an admirer of the king as photos of a visit to his supposed grave site in the Quedlinburg cathedral on the occasion of Heinrich's 1,000 anniversary of his death on July 2, 1936 document [the grave was possibly that of a female saint; See, 344 f.]), thus, based on today's factual situation individual Kersten's statements may, in detail, be in doubt. However, since the statements to Himmler's inclination to the occult agree in most part with those of his astrologer, Wilhelm Wulff, and, in part, are supported by Himmler's, today available, secret speeches, the inclusion of the occultist Karl-Maria Wiligut into the SS and the analysis of the literature read by him, his statements are, in my opinion, to this point, quotable. For a critique of Kersten's credibility see: [Jong, Louis de, article: "Hat Felix Kersten das niederländishe Volk gerettet?", in: Wilhelm, 77 ff.] De Jong explains: "As a result of the investigation of this work it can indeed be stated that Kersten truly engaged himself for the release of Dutch and other prisoners or condemned. Also, Kersten's important mediator function re the transport of the above mentioned thousand Dutch women to Sweden stands without question, just as his part in the measures Himmler exacted during the final phase of the war to save the lives of several thousand Jews. Finally, it is also certain that Kersten risked his life in these efforts." [Wilhelm, 83] De Jong proves that Kersten, with reference to the supposed deportation plan for the Dutch – according to Kersten, they were to be settled in the East – numerous factual mistakes, inconsistencies, and even document forgings. About the Kersten author Besgen, Jong explains: "In the bibliography Besgen lists 'Kersten's Diary from 1939-1945, 807 pages long' ... Possibly, Besgen counted the pages found in notes of and about Kersten in the Rijksinstituut voor Oorlogsdocumenttatie ... However, the Rijksinstituut des not possess a 'Diary' of Kersten's of 807 pages ... the 'Diary' found in Kersten's estate has only 87 pages." Nevertheless, Kersten's statements seem to contain possess true core, however, no direct deportation plan. De Jong: "It can be assumed that already by the end of 1940 or the beginning of 1941 it had become known to Kersten that the department of the RKF assumed that, after all, several millions of Dutch and Flemish were already in eastern Europe – not following direct pressure, but as a result of propaganda and an artificially, low-kept living standard in the Netherlands and Belgium." [Wilhelm, 136] De Jong about Kersten's statements: "However, a rule of his communications is that they have a certain touch (sometimes strong, sometimes weak) with reality ... Whatever caused Kersten to invent the deportation plan is not exactly known ... The main motive was surely the situation, in which Kersten found himself in Sweden in the summer of 1945. Kersten had substantially contributed to the Swedish government's permission to pursue an action in Germany during the final phase of the war, by which many thousands of prisoners from concentration camps were brought in busses to Sweden ... None of the assistants [of the, on the Swedish side, officially mediating Count] Bernadotte were named, neither Kersten ... Not for nothing was Kersten deeply disappointed ... and that in a situation when a part of Swedish public opinion made a stand against the 'Nazi' Felix Kersten ... It is understandable that Kersten felt so acutely threatened in Sweden that his hopes for help became directed to the Netherlands ... Of course, he knew that no one would accept the new story just like that. Therefore, the

nated Himmler, but also the possibilities of clairvoyance and telepathy. In 1923, he occupied himself with the "Second Sight." This terminology – the ability for clairvoyance – is mainly used in Scotland and in Westfalia as "Spökenkiekerei" (Ghost sight)). With this, gifted young, and also older people, are able to perceive future accidents photo-realistically or, at least, acoustically, e.g. in the form of day dreams. It was mostly burning houses or funerals of which they subsequently reported. As a rule, this gift is considered an unpleasant burden by the affected persons and is often kept secret. Friedrich zur Bonsen, who wrote a treatise on the subject that was read by Himmler in 1923, reported, for instance, on a particular case. The above cited author of the "Theory of Spirit Knowledge," the ophtamologist and Swedenborg/Mesmer-adept Johann Heinrich Jung-Stilling wrote:

"A case of this nature, the noble Jung-Stilling (+1817), highly valued by Goethe, claimed expressly to be able to vouch for. It occurred in County Mark. A 'Seer' had disclosed to the pastor of the Protestant parish that he would soon accompany a corpse from his own house. Since the pastor's wife was suffering from health problems, fright and displeasure of the latter was so great that he chased the man away. Suddenly, the housemaid died. Following custom, the pastor, as master of the house, would now have had to accompany the coffin, walking alongside it; but in order to prevent the fulfillment of the vision but, on the other hand, not to hurt the relatives of the deceased, he made his by now recovered wife assume his position in the funeral procession. The moment the procession started to move, the woman passed out, falling to the ground, and the frightened pastor now no longer hesitated to assume his assigned position behind the coffin."[1]

Zur Bonsen did not leave it solely with the depiction of dozens of cases; he also presented diverse contemporary attempts at explaining clairvoyance, for instance du Prel's explanation: "Du Prel, a (Darwinist), one of the main representatives of spirit knowledge in Germany, seeks to explain the appearances by a second paranormal I that was effective in human beings, going beyond self-awareness. The more the sensory awareness was suppressed, the stronger it stirred … The … Westfalian doctor Sebregondi attempted already in 1840 to explain sighting by a singular appearance. It was to proceed from the so-called public spirit which one could possibly call the sixth sense. This [public spirit is] … effective in

---

'proofs.'" [de Jong, 136 ff.] Also Michael Kater, Josef Ackermann, and Peter Padfield [Padfield, viii] refer repeatedly to Kersten.

1   Bonsen, 72

giving, beyond space and time, a preview of the universe and to see things that will possibly occur in the future: 'An outflow of infinite, hidden power.' Just as a common sensory perception requires a means, e.g. for the process of seeing light, thus it employs also a means, which, however, 'was supposed to be even more subtle in movement and faster than light,' this being an outflow from the nervous system. This is the so-called organic ether, that supposed nerve radiation (Od), whose existence wonderfully effects spiritualism, as is known, which also claims ... 'Now, to explain the sightings, we must assume that the soul by means of the sense of public spirit and organic ether gets in touch with the universe through a to us, of course, not in a sensory representable means, and from there obtains the message that lies outside the circle of common knowledge and steps beyond the limitations of the finality of space and time.'" However, zur Bonsen looked skeptically at these attempts at explanation: "The assumption is just as daring and without proof as is the explanation for thought transmission by ether waves emanating from the brain."[1] He also reported events which suggested a transmission of visions to other people present in the room: "The belief in the peculiar transmission of the second sight from the seer to someone present is still widely accepted in Westfalia ... However, we reserve judgment since verification by flawless self-witnessing is impossible."[2] Although zur Bonsen doubted that either approach served as an explanation, he did not deny the phenomenon as such. Thus, he writes towards the end of his exposition: "[The reality of second sight] is after all proof for the spiritual essence and immortality for the soul"[3] "Since the beginning, when, in the inanimate nature surrounding us, forces and laws ruled, we, until now, were unaware of their nature like electricity, still is in the present. When others, like Röntgen radiation and radium, have become known to us only now, yes, ... it is no different from the forces and abilities of the soul." "Everything finite is confined in space and time. Since the soul is by clairvoyance capable of rising beyond both these limitations, its sight is able to leave both behind, and it therefore follows that it is itself not finite, but infinite and indestructable."[4] Here again, the belief in the beyond breaks through, as du Prel has already referred to it as being "spiritual optimism." Himmler commented on his reading experience of the text about the "Second Sight": "It is

---

1  Bonsen, 91 ff.
2  Bonsen, 88 f. – Zur Bonsen refers also to the Second Face, which old popular belief granted dogs and horses, for instance, in the case of earth quakes and solar eclipses. [Bonsen, 114]
3  Bonsen, 115 f.
4  Bonsen, 120

an exact report and collection of unknown and incredible areas, a small section of the infinite *terra incognita*, everything extrasensory, including astrology, hypnosis, spiritualism, telepathy, etc. – representation and attempts at explanation, scientific, and easily understood."[1]

In 1866, the founder of a vegetarian sect, Otto Hanisch, was born in western Prussia, the son of a German-Russian railroad official. The family subsequently emigrated to America. There, in Chicago, Hanisch founded in 1899 the Mazdaznan Movement under the name of Otoman Zar-Adusht Hanish. The name was meant to mean "Master Thought" and refers to the Persian Light god Ahura Mazda. Donations financed the building of a Mazdaznan temple. By reverting to the Persian-Zoroastric Zend Avesta and clichés from far-east religions, rules for the maintenance of meat and the abstenance of alcohol and tobacco were developed. The eastern pure incarnation and karma teachings were also integrated with reference to modern evolutionary theory. Added were breathing exercises, for the "basis of physical as well as mental development formed by conscious breathing." For missionary work in German-speaking countries, the Mazdaznan delegate David Ammann was dispatched who, in 1907, began his activities with the founding of the "Zarathustra Organization" in Leipzig. Leipzig became, after Chicago, the second Mazdaznan Center. In 1912, there existed already 33 Mazdaznan circles on German territory. The, at most, 1,000 members of the movement must have come especially from the educated citizenship, or, as it was said in a respective announcement: "the better classes" (artists, writers, musicians, professors). In 1913, the true identity and origin of Hanisch, who had been treated as the son of the Russian General Consul in Teheran and an Iranian princess, became public in a judicial hearing. In the course of this trial, he was sentenced for the circulation of lascivious publications. The "Hammer," published by the anti-semite, Theodor Fritsch, contributed to the disclosure of Hanisch's true identity. Fritsch who also was fishing in gnostic waters, was annoyed by the US-comptetition, as well as other established life reformers who saw in the Mazdaznan movement only a dangerous "freeloader." Amman, was expelled from Saxony as an "annoying foreigner," and had to move to Switzerland. In Herligberg near Zurich, he founded an international Mazdaznan college. Following the seizure of power by the National Socialists, the movement was prohibited. Otto Hanisch died 1936 in Los Angeles.[2]

---

1   Himmler, Leseliste, Title 175
2   Krabbe, "Exkurs: Mazdaznan," 73 ff.

In 1919 a book was published in Basel by Karl Heise, entitled "The Entente-Freemason and World War, a contribution to the History of the World War and Understanding of True Freemasonry." Heise tried to prove in his anti-semitically-colored, conspiracy-theory work that Freemasonry staged the first World War.[1] Heise was a member of the Guido-von-List Organization and a leading personality of the Zurich Mazdaznan cult.[2] Together with his brother, Heinrich Heise, he operated the commune "Aryana" near Zurich.[3]

In 1921, Heise published a second book with a similar aim – claiming anew in "Occult Lodges": "It is and remains a fact that the entire war politics originated from the secret activities of certain occult Lodge circles,"[4] Heise's world view follows a classic black-and-white scheme. The leader of the evil Occultists, 'on the left hand,' is the "field commander of the dark assemblies." He fights the good Occultists 'on the right hand.' This, explains Heise, is why France repeatedly attacks Germany: "One can really understand the entire situation if, again and again, one reminds oneself of the 'Soldiers of the Field Commander': of those 'Brothers of Shadow,' who, for hundreds of years live side-by-side with the 'Brothers of Light' and try to thwart everything of beneficial nature that the latter want to bring to humanity."[5] With it, he follows the classic dualism of the gnostic manichaism, which is also mentioned: "Manichaism knew how to properly connect the pre- and post-Christian mysteries. However, it was implacably pursued and almost entirely exterminated by the sailing under the dark, occult rule of the 'Church,' which is then why the Rosenkreuzer grouping began its silent efficacy ... In the 9th century, the Church thought to have this 'heresy' eliminated. That is when, silently arose the communities of the Katharer, Albigenser, Johannites, Templeirons and Templellords, which carried Manichaism into modern Freemasonry!"[6] Unfortunately, sections of Freemasonry were now controlled by the evil Occultists. But, whoever looks, shall find: "An immense wisdom of the deepest things of life is kept. Of it, we find a rich measure in the Freemason documents. But covered by the dust of centuries ... Sometimes, an intuitive 'brother' softly lifts the lid of the ark of the covenant just a little and sees wonders ... The majority of 'insiders,' who are themselves anointed with occult practices are looking – into the void. We know that ... in world-controlling

---

1     Rudolf Steiner is positively mentioned by Heise in "Okkultes Logentum." [Heise, 2, 80]
2     Goodrick-Clarke, 43-45
3     Goodrick-Clarke, 55
4     Heise, 1
5     Heise, 22
6     Heise, 15

England ... the leading politicians ... [are] occultist – of course not on the Right Hand."[1] These politicians follow a dangerous, "blurred gnosticism."[2] Supposedly, they are supported by the "dark Mahatmas"[3] and the spirits of deceased British generals: "Every occultist knows the so-called textbook, in which the thoughts of all living and once-living have been entered by the so-called 'Lipikas' or Guardians of Souls (the 'Writers of Osiris'). Following specific occult practices to be performed, these special 'Stanza' can be read like any other physically available book. And from this occult 'text' the 'Insiders on the Left Hand' confront all the Cromwells and Nelsons ... who, earlier had already whipped up England to the subjugation of the world." Thus it happens "that the 'dead' point the way to world hegemony."[4] "The true lodges (not the pseudo-lodges, who are like sand by the sea) have, since they are invited from the mental, spiritual world to the 'table of King Arthur' ... at any time knowledge of that which must necessarily happen in the world for the 'Brothers', i.e. the greater humanity."[5]

At this point, may a small digression to King Arthur's legendary table round with the twelve knights (mentioned by Heise) and the Wewelsburg of the SS be permitted and presented? In 1933, Himmler looked, as Lange extensively states, for a suitable castle in Westfalia for the planned SS-Reichsführer-School. According to Karl Wolff, Head of the Personal Staff of the SS-Reichsführer. The occultist Wiligut pointed out the Wewelsburg near Paderborn to Himmler.[6] To this – following the not always reliable statements of Wolff's – an old prophesy of the "Battle at the Birkenbaum," is supposed to have contributed, according to which an army from the East had been destroyed near a Westfalian castle. The battle had already been cited in the above-mentioned book of zur Bonsen's, which Himmler had read. It is also dealt with in a book of Bender's "Does the Battle at the Birkenbaum lie ahead?," which Himmler also read according to his reading list in 1926. In 1937, Himmler declared in his speech at the Groupleader-Conference in Bad Tölz: "I will hang ... in the Wewelsburg, in the hall of the group leaders ... the coat of arms of the deceased group leaders, so that those following us, are always advised before our tables ..."[7] The former secret service head, Walter Schellenberg, reported of disciplinary court proceedings against the

---

1     Heise, 28
2     Heise, 31
3     Heise, 29
4     Heise, 74
5     Heise, 36
6     Lange, Wiligut, 276
7     cited after Lange, Wiligut, 281

supreme commander of the army, Colonel General Freiherr von Fritsch: "Here I accidentally became a witness of an occult quirk of Himmler's, with which he even busied the leader of the SS. During the proceedings against Fritsch, he had ordered about twelve of his most trusted SS-leaders to a room adjacent to the hearing room and had ordered them to impart a suggestive influence by will of concentration on the accused colonel general. Himmler was convinced that, under this influence, the accused would have to tell the truth … Thus, the SS-organization was established by him following the principles of the Jesuit Order … Near Paderborn, he had refurbished a Middle-Age castle, the so-called Wewelsburg – it was, so to speak, the great 'SS-monastery,' where the order's general summoned once annually the Secret Assembly."[1] Lange mentions that the Group-Headleader-Hall of the castle was decorated with twelve stone columns arranged in a circle with marble inlay work on the floor, representing a circular symbol whose spokes consisted of twelve jagged Sig-runes.[2] As an explanation for this marble-fashioned symbol, I do not exclude it being an Islamic ornamental pattern. Guénon writes of this – often in the sacral area and almost everywhere to be found –"12": "It is in any case conspicuous that several authors confirm with assurance that the true Rosenkeuzer left Europe shortly after the Thirty-Years-War, to retreat to Asia. To this may be mentioned that there were twelve Rosenkreuz adepts, the same number we find again in the innermost circle of the Agartha as well as the constitution of so many spiritual centers, which are a representation of this highest of centers."[3] However, a more banal explanation must be considered: In 1953, Kersten wrote about Himmler: "His great round visitor's table in Berlin was known. Twelve people was the largest number admitted, just as with the legendary King Arthur."[4] Himmler may have received the inspiration to copy him by reading Heise's text "King Arthur's Table," in the Wewelsburg, where the "real" lodges were to find seats in a spiritual world. However, all attempts at explanation must remain speculative, and, therefore, short of productive sources.

Heise writes that he had earlier already identified plenty of references in the publication "Zentralblatt für Okkultismus."[5] "If modern man loses his final hold, which he can only find in a pure, spiritually-lead Christianity … – through

---

[1] Schellenberg, Walter: Aufzeichnungen, Wiesbaden 1979, cited after Lange, Wiligut, 280
[2] Lange, Wiligut, 278
[3] Guénon, König, 63
[4] Kersten, 392
[5] Heise, 16

today's Buddhism no one [arrives] any more at the comprehension of the high sense and spirit that is inherent in the thought of the Maitreya-Buddha as the 'Accomplisher of Christianity' – then, the destruction without end, the fight of all against all, is the end result."[1] Heise reports of two kinds of spiritual training with, at a time, different endings: One leading to philanthropy by means of "loosening and rejuvenating of the physical body-uplifting Image-power body, the, in the physical body acting ether-body." The other was to cause misanthropy by a "hardening of the ether body."[2] He pointed out that "a professor, Elmar Gates, had conducted tests in his laboratory to demonstrate 'the departure of the ether body in killed rats,' while in Edison's laboratory live rabbits were being killed by electric current, then 'revived again' by electric current. Of this nature are occult practices, which the victors in the great World War seemingly intent to introduce, put into effect in human life … these methods … do not lead to gnosis …"[3] Heise also claims to know, when the "dark magicians" plan their next coup against humanity. He wrote in 1921: "The occult phenomena become that much more questionable when precisely these dark magicians declare the year 1932, or 1956, respectively, as the point in time for which they offer some obscure being of humanity as the incarnated (false) Messiah … a prophet of their devilish world!"[4]

Himmler commented on Heise's book with the words: "A deeply serious text that makes one suspect much. There is a good and bad principle, which acts and makes itself felt in human societies."[5] In 1940, Himmler, according to his massage therapist, Kersten, elaborated about the prohibition of national lodges:

"All lodges have secret superiors who control those that are externally visible. Do I know who truly stands behind a conventional doctor as the Chair Master? … Next to the Supreme Master, who is required as the poster image, sits an inconspicuous man who, in reality, holds a much higher lodge rank within World-Freemasonry, and with mastery handles the system of 'Shadowing' according to instructions. Only one power has not been deceived, the Catholic Church. It is a fierce enemy of every lodge … The Church knows why it is so unrelenting. It works itself following lodge principles, its orders, especially the Jesuit Orders, are nothing else … It knows what it itself has accomplished by

---

1 Heise, 19
2 Heise, 69
3 Heise, 75
4 Heise, 90
5 Himmler, Reading list, page 39, Title No. 258, read February 1926

this lodge system, it does not tolerate any opposition lodge ... However, one ought not to be led astray by the explanation that the Church is hostile to the lodges because they pay homage to liberal ideas."[1] Here, Himmler justified the prohibition of lodge membership of the Catholics with the lodge attachment of the Church. Parallel to it, his excursus of the prohibition of the national lodges close to the National Socialists becomes a confession for the lodge attachment of the SS. At that it did not address a textual delimitation but the question of the power monopoly.

That Himmler had not only in his early times been interested in the passive consumption of occult theses, but also in the practical application of occult knowledge, shows, next to the "Pendulum Practice," the following letter dated 1925.

"Heinrich Himmler
Graduate in Agriculture
Landshut, Sept. 11, 25
Seligenthalerstr. 11/I

Mr. Professor Heilmaier
Munich
Reitmorstr. 26/IV right

Highly esteemed Mr. Professor!

Allow me to approach you today with a question.

Are you familiar with the 'League of the Good' and its endeavors? It is lead by a man writing under the alias *Weishaar*. I am not certain what I am to think in particular of the publication of the horoscope of the delegate, Jürgen von Ramin's.[2] Something like this cannot readily be checked here, and I see from

---

[1] Kersten, 32
[2] With Jürgen von Ramin we are dealing with an author of diverse racist articles on the subject of nobility and race: Ramin, Jürgen v.: "Berufung" (Reference) [Gleichschaltung, "Geist von Potsdam"], Essay, Deutsches Adelsblatt. Magazine of the German Adelsgenossenschaft, year LI. (1933), pages 297-298; Ramin, Jürgen v.: "Kampf dem Bolschewismus", Essay, Deutsches Adelsblatt, year LI. (1933), pages 165-166' Ramin, Jürgen v., author of article ("Auslese oder Clique?") of thought about race in connection with nobility 1934, German Fed. Archives (BArch) Berlin Lichterfelde, Section Reich, File signature: R8034 II no. 8597, fol. 159 a back page; Ramin, Jürgen v., author of article ("Mitleid und

```
Heinrich Himmler
Dipl.-Landwirt                                      Landshut, 11.9.25.
                                                    Seligenthalerstr. 11/I.

      Herrn
      Professor H e i l m a i e r
                                                    M ü n c h e n ,
                                                    Reitmorstr. 26/IV rechts


                  Hochverehrter Herr Professor!
            Gestatten Sie,daß ich heute mit einer Frage an Sie heran
tete.
            Sind Sie über den "Bund der Guten" u. seine Bestrebungen
unterrichtet? Er ist geführt von einem Mann, der unter dem Decknamen
W e i s h a a r   schreibt. Ich bin mir nicht recht im Klaren was ich
namentlich über die Veröffentlichung des Horoskops des Abg. Jürgen
von Ramin halten soll. So etwas läßt sich hier zu wenig nachprüfen
und ich sehe darin die Möglichkeit, Menschen, die einem unbequem sind
durch Veröffentlichung solcher Horoskope unmöglich zu ma-
chen. Sollten Sie den Bund noch nicht kennen, so bin ich gerne bereit
Ihnen Schriften davon zu übersenden.
            Würde mich sehr freuen Sie u. Ihren
Freund, Hrn. P f a f f e n z e l l e r   in München einmal treffen kön-
te. Ich hoffe schon kann ich mit Pfaffenzeller, wenn der Landtag wieder
angegangen ist, einmal etwas ausmachen.
```

Heinrich Himmler's letter to the Munich Astrologer Heilmaier 1925 (German Federal Archives) – due to the thinness of the paper the text on the reverse page shines through)

it the possibility of compromising irksome people by the publication of a bad horoscope. Should you not yet have knowledge of this League, I will be pleased to forward you publications about it.

I would be pleased if I could at some time meet with you and your friend, Mr. *Pfaffenzeller,* in Munich. I think that once the parliament is in session again, I can arrange something with Mr. Pfaffenzeller.

Looking forward to your kind response, I am with loyal German greeting!
Your very devoted
H.H.

P.S. Would you be willing to cast a horoscope for me based on the following birth dates?
Munich Oct. 7, 1900 4-1/4 afternoon
Landshut Sept. 27.1903 8 h morning
Regensburg Mar. 2, 1903 3/4 5 afternoon
Schwetzingen near Heidelberg Apr. 3. 1896 1 h night"[1]

The reply of "Studienrat C. HEILMAIER Munich," who, was also obviously engaged as an astrologer on the side, required eight days and certainly must not have been satisfactory to Himmler:

"Very honored Mister HIMMLER!
... With respect to your question re the 'League of the Good,' I am unable to provide you with any information, however, the name itself suffices for a judgment. A piece of folk wisdom has long since issued the correct judgment on self-adulation ... When [everyone] ... at all times fulfills that which he owes everyone of his fellow men without difference in education or the caste he belongs to, and what he reasonably demands at all times for himself, then his inner senses awaken, and he no longer requires horoscopes with which he

---

Notwendigkeit"), about "Self Cleansing" of the German Adelsgenossenschaft of "blood aliens" 1934, Fed. Archives, File signature: R8034 II no. 8597, fol. 161.; Commented by the chief executive officer of the German Adelsgenossenschaft, v. Bogen ("Mitleid und Notwendigkeit") 1934, Fed. Arch., Section Reich, File signature: R8034 II no. 8597, fol. 161/162; Galen-Enniger, Graf v. / Ramin, Jürgen v., / Eulenburg, Antonie Gräfin zu / Stolberg-Wernigerode, Gräfin zu, Mentioned in an article the marriage of a Countess zu Eulenburg to the Jew Hirsch and reaction of Count Galen ("Verrat oder Dummheit?") 1934, Fed. Arch. File signature: R8034 II no. 8597, fol. 179

1   German Fed. Archives, Nachlass Himmler, N 1126, NL 126/17

intends quite possibly to check and grill his fellow-workers ... To provide you with horoscopes for the data transmitted, I would also not be in the position to provide due to the fact that a thoroughly cast H. ... would require a good three days work, which, aside from my professional and extra-professional work, cannot be considered. You will therefore not take it as unfriendly that I cannot meet your request for the 4 horoscopes.

With excellent respect
devoted Karl Heilmaier"[1]

Among the birth dates Himmler supplied to Heilmaier for the casting of horoscopes is also his own birth date (Oct. 7, 1900). Heilmaier, obviously assumed that Himmler wants to learn more about "possible fellow-workers" by means of the horoscopes.

The mentioned leader of the "League of the Good" is Kurt Paehlke ("Weishaar / "Whitehair"), who appeared in publication titles such as "The World Judgment" (1932). The name of his organization, "League of the Good (Guoten)," is derived from the "Good" as well as the "Goth." The League and numerous attached organizations distributed, especially in East Prussia, the long-standing seat of the League, ariosophic-gnostic thought.[2] Following his own statements, they included the, for the understanding of League texts, necessary "knowledge areas": "Racial knowledge, Theosophy, Occultism, Astrology, the secret teachings of various kinds (e.g. Kaballa, Teachings of Freemasonry), and the research results of the latest sciences."[3] According to National-Socialist data, the membership culminated in 3,000 people.[4] The secret society developed race-gnostic human breeding visions and began with their practical application.

---

1  German Fed. Archives, Nachlass Himmler, N 1126, NL 126/17
2  Glowka, 3, 28
3  "Rd.", Article: "Der Bund der Guoten und 'Die innere Mission in Ostpreußen'," in: Der Femstern, no. 11-12, 21. Wonnemond, 1926, 3 (130). – The author reacted to a critical essay with the title "Der Bund der Guten" in the publication "Die innere Mission in Ostpreußen."
4  Acc. to the state police office of the administrative district Königsberg, the number of BDG and DHO members, even still in 1937, "amounts to thousands here in East Prussia." [Anschreiben Preußisch-Geheime Staatspolizei, Staatspolizeistelle für den Regierungsbezirk Königsberg an die Geheime Staatspolizei, Geheimes Staatspolizeiamt, Ref. II C 2 B, z.H. SS-Standartenführer Müller oder Vertreter im Amt, Berlin, Prinz-Albrecht-Str. 8 of March 24, 1937, klassifiziert "Geheim!," page 11, in: Fed. Arch. R58 file 7275, Bund der Guoten] 1941 it states retrospectively: "During the years 1924 to 1928 membership reached a maximum of about 3,000; 4/5 of the members lived in East Prussia." [Letter

At first, its leader Paehlke sought an alliance with the emergent National Socialist party, but then stumbled over a meeting with opponents within the NS-party in Berlin in 1933 and over own resistance activities that became known to the intelligence service. This background, in combination with the NS-efforts to keep lodge-similar competition beyond its own SS-order at bay, led finally to that Paehlke was several times imprisoned in concentration camps where he does not seem have survived to the end of the war.[1] What Adolf Lanz had been for Vienna and Alfred Schuler[2] for Munich with respect to the spreading of neo-gnostic ideas, Paehlke was to represent for East Prussia.

What actually is Gnosis? And what connected Himmler to this belief?

An old religio-philosophical movement, gnosis was crossed in the 19th century with the then new hereditary theories. The dominating model of gnosis is the light, from which the gnostic thinks to have emerged, whose divine part he thinks to be, and to which he imagines to return. The realization of one's own divinity, the divine light as a spark of one's own soul, is called "Gnosis" (realization). Differentiated were – depending on the light's strength – three groups of people: 1) People who carried especially strong light in themselves, 2) People whose divine share of light was less, and 3) People who did not hold any light, i.e. who were bound to the material. This old threefold division in groups of people was now applied to races of people: Light-blond northern Europeans with light-blue eyes were counted as god-people with the greatest share of light. Half-castes were already exposed to the process of light-loss, since their blood that had been identified as being the carrier of light-substance, and was already, following these teachings, a mixture. Jews counted as being matter-bound and light-less. Once the quality of a soul had been tied to a physical substance, the spiritual upgrading of humanity could, following these teachings, best be accomplished by means of physical pure-breeding – as was sufficiently known from

---

of SS-Obersturmführer Spengler to the Chief of Security police of the SD, Berlin April 1, 1941 for the Highest Party Court of the NSDAP, Munich; Fed.Arch R 187 219, fol. 1 Slg. Schumacher, pages 11-13] Ruhnau estimates membership substantially lower at 300-500 persons. [phone conversation with Dietrich Ruhnau on Febr. 11, 2005] In light of the fact that Paehlke in a letter bemoaned the loss of 1,000 members, the NS-specifications are clearly more probable. Paehlke wrote: "In our lists 1,000 members have been deleted, it being the indication that they had been wrongly entered ... ["Duplicate of a certified duplicate. Letter of the Master to Eilimar; Kamben, 26th of the Easter month 1928, in: Fed. Arch. R 58 File 7275, Bund der Guoten, page 39 ff.]

1   See Wegener, Weishaar und der Geheimbund der Guoten
2   Wegener, Schuler. Mohler opines: "From a distance, Schuler had become more and more visible as one of the great underground stimulators." [Mohler, 47]

Der Reichsführer-ℋ  
Tgb.Nr. AR/2778  
RF/Gr.

Berlin, den 13. März 1937.

An den  
Chef des Rasse- und Siedlungshauptamtes,  
<u>Berlin</u>

1.) Ich bitte, ℋ-Hauptsturmführer Lienau zu verbieten, dass er weiter auf dem Gebiet der Freimaurerei schriftstellerisch arbeitet.

2.) Ich wünsche nicht, dass das von ihm bearbeitete Schulungsmaterial über Freimaurerei herausgegeben wird. Hersteller von Schulungsmaterial über unsere Gegner ist <u>nur</u> das SD-Hauptamt.

3.) Ich ersuche, Lienau zu veranlassen, dass er die gegenüber der Edda-Gesellschaft und dem verstorbenen Vorsitzenden Rudolf, John von Gorsleben gemachten Anwürfe gegenüber dem jetzigen Vorsitzenden der Edda-Gesellschaft, Herrn von Bülow, zurücknimmt.  
Ich habe veranlasst, dass das Büchlein von Lienau nicht eingezogen wird; ich wünsche jedoch keine Neuauflage. Was Gorsleben angeht, so kannte ich den Mann persönlich sehr genau und habe die Überzeugung, dass er von Jesuiten umgebracht worden ist. Es ist ein völlig falscher Standpunkt von Lienau, alle Dinge, die vielleicht einen etwas mystischen Inhalt haben, als Freimaurerei anzusehen, da er dabei völlig vergisst, dass grosse Teile des sogenannten Geistesgutes der Freimaurerei germanischen Ursprungs sind und unseren Vorfahren gestohlen wurden. Insgesamt bitte ich, ihn darüber zu belehren, dass er mit blossen Behauptungen und Anstänkern anderer Leute der Bekämpfung unserer Gegner nicht dient und Deutschland keinen Nutzen bringt.

Der Reichsführer-ℋ  
H. Himmler

Himmler: "Concerning Gorsleben, I knew this man personally very well ..." (Ger. Fed. Arch.)

biology, medicine, and agriculture: The physical destruction of carriers of the light-less blood and "Outmendeling" of the already partly less-lighted half-castes by crossing with purebred light carriers. This action seemed suited to vanquish the opponent of the light-god of gnosis, the god of darkness, and to attain with it an important win on points in the dualistic-manichaen cosmic battle. The result of this connection of religious philosophy and hereditary teachings was a race politics that found its master in Adolf Lanz, a failed Zisterzienser monk from Austria and, to this day, carries the name of ariosophy.

By the instrument of reuniting the blonds and the means of racial inbreeding the light content of the people, imagined long-term over generations, was to be enriched again until its result would equal the once lost ideal conditions (like Atlantis): A nordic, purebred people, light-blond gods with supernatural abilities. This already becomes clear in the 1918 novel of the settlement planner and Lanz-Order-Brother, Detlef Schmude, who put in the neighborhood of a forest chapel of the Tempel-Irons, a (ficticious) race settlement: "[Here] gradually grew people, who without any difference of rank and professional activity found, entirely according to their desire, access to the teachings of the initiates. Almost all engaged mostly in agriculture and the trades related to it … Taking the unshakable laws of nature into account, the [Order prior Victor] knew that only in the third or forth generation could the highest goal of total dominance of the device be reached in us."[1]

Lanz's teachings found fast distribution by people attached to him, who were organized in the *Ordo Novi Templi*, the New-Templar Order, founded by him.[1] A member of this order by name of Fra Rig (Fra = Frater = Brother), was Rudolf John Gorsleben, the later "chancellor" of the Edda Society, Munich.[2] In March of 1937, when the Edda Society became suspected of Freemasonry, Himmler held his hand protectively over this society. He dressed down the SS-Hauptsturmführer Walter Lienau, who, in his propaganda text "Of Freemasonry and Lodges" (1936) had raised the suspicion not only of an organizational but also of contentional proximity to Freemasonry, against the Edda Society, and, in a letter he wrote to the Head of the Race- and Settlement-Main-Office, Walther Darré: "1) I request to forbid SS-Hauptsturmführer Lienau to continue writing on the subject of Freemasonry. 2) I do not wish to have the educational mate-

---

1   Schmude, Gedichte (Poems), 60 f., 64
2   Mohler, 355; Gorsleben (March 16, 1883 - Aug. 23, 1930); The list of 73 verifiable members of the O.N.T. order is found with Hieronimus. Hieronimus: "Even at its best time, the order may not have more than 300-400 members." [Hieronimus, 25 ff.]

rial he has worked on published. Producer of educational material about our opponents is only the SD-Main Office. 3) I request to have Lienau retract the accusations he has made against the Edda Society and the deceased chairman Rudolf, John von Gorsleben, and the current chairman of the Edda Society, Mr. von Bülow. I have arranged for Lienau's booklet not to be withdrawn, but do not wish for a new edition. Concerning Gorsleben, I knew this man personally very well and am convinced that he was killed by Jesuits. Lienau's position is totally wrong in that he sees all things that may have some mystic content as Freemasonry, at which he totally forgets that large parts of the so-called mental values of Freemasonry are of Germanic origin, stolen from our ancestors. In total, I request to instruct him that his mere claims and accusations of other people do not serve to fight our opponents and do not bring anything useful to Germany. The Reichsführer-SS H. Himmler."[1]

Himmler's sympathy for the Edda Society, founded by the Lanz-follower Gorsleben, was not new: Already ten years earlier, on August 13, 1926, Himmler transferred 2 Reichsmark to the Rudolf John Gorsleben Edda Society, Dinkelsbühl, possibly for a newspaper of the Society.[2] Unfortunately, no purpose can be drawn from the respective proof-of-mail delivery.

---

[1] Germ.Fed.Arch, RS Walter Lienau, born June 5, 1906. A Thank You to Thomas Hauer for the tip!

[2] Certificate of mailing of Postscheckamt Munich of August 13, 1926, Fed. Arch., Estate Himmler, N 1126, NL 126/2

# 6 The Stars: Wilhelm Wulff

A further confirmation of Himmler's occult obsession are the events surrounding his astrologer, Wilhelm Wulff, whose memoirs were published in 1968. As a result of Hess' flight to England – he was widely known to believe in the stars – numerous astrologers were imprisoned in 1941 and taken to concentration camps. Nevertheless, Wulff was exempted from admission to a concentration camp in order to remain available to advise Himmler and other NS-Greats of Himmler's surroundings. In his memoirs, Wulff describes the visit of a research group "SP" (possibly meaning "Sideric Pendulum"), which, supposedly, was placed under the auspices of the Supreme Command of the Navy (OKM): "Half a year after my release from the concentration camp Fuhlsbüttel, I was, sometime in March of 1942, ordered to a totally unknown institute in Berlin as a scientific assistant. This was prompted by the Nuremberg astronomer and astrologer Dr. Wilhelm Hartmann, a friend of mine. I traveled to Berlin and introduced myself at the Research Institute of the OKM ... This division, inside the Navy, was led by a captain. The activities of the research institute were top secret. The captain's subordinates were a strange group: There were spiritual media and psychics – what the sciences call people who are especially sensitive to psychic influences –, there were pendulum operators (persons, who knew how to work with the sideric pendulum), Tattwa-researchers (followers of a type of Indian pendulum teaching), astrologers and astronomers, ballisticers and mathematicians. From the highest circles of the Navy – OKM – the institute had the assignment of tracing the enemy's convoys to ascertain their torpedoing by German U-boat flotillas. Day by day, the pendulum operators pored over marine maps with arms outstretched."[1]

In 1943, according to Wulff's own statements, he was to help find Mussolini who had disappeared in Italy: "I was introduced to the Regierungsrat [senior civil servant] Lobbes and later to the Head of the Reichskriminalpolizeiamt, Arthur Nebe, who gave me the following orders from Himmler: I was to search immediately for Mussolini, who, at the time, had disappeared as a result of the Badoglio-action ... When I returned to Berlin, I received Nebe's assignment to work with 25 birth dates of high Nazi-leaders that were supplied to me, which were pointed out to me as being corruption cases ... When I turned in my

---

1   Wulff, 113 f. For this event about the OKM see also: Walther, Gerda: Zum anderen Ufer – Vom Marxismus and Atheismus zum Christentum, Remagen 1960, 599 ff. [as per Wulff, 113]

work … I had a clash with Himmler's aide-de-camp Suchanek, who thought I had not been fast enough. Suchanek explained: 'The Reichsführer ask that you must work faster, put in a greater effort, or it could happen that you will end up like Goldmacher Tausend,[1] who now sits in the KZ and will sit there until he can make gold'"[2] This point of Wulff's is also taken up by Michael Kater for his historical study on the SS-Association Ahnenerbe [Ancestral Heredity].[3]

---

1  See Wegener, Franz: Der Alchemist Franz Tausend. Alchemie und Nationalsozialismus

2  Wulff, 126 f.; 221 – However, with Wulff several statements are found which appear exaggerated or unrealistic, such as Himmler is supposed to have told him about a car accident with the words: "On this day I drove my car in the dark myself, missed the road and dropped down a 40 meter high slope onto the tracks of the Schwarzwaldbahn, precisely at the moment when the train was coming. Only with an effort were we able to save ourselves. – It is peculiar how correct the horoscope is." [Wulff, 192] – It must be doubted that a crash from a height of 40(!) meters took place. Wulff's comments about the development and testing [!] of atomic weapons sound unbelievable. [Wulff, 202] It raises the question how Wulff's statements on this subject in 1968 could pass the Bertelsmann Publisher's editorial department without objection. But since Wulff's statements in many points concerning Himmler's occult tendencies match those of Himmler's massage therapist Kersten, as well as Himmler's assessments in his own reading list re occult titles, I think him – as I do Kater – on these items quotable. To Bormann's request 1941, the State Police ought to move against astrologers, occultists, spiritualists, anthrosophes, theosophes, ariosophes, etc, see: Himmler, Service calendar, 170, footnote 14. Stutterheim writes to it: "Only 1942, after Rudolf Hess's flight to England a main department 'Occultism' was established in the NSDAP main office for people's health under the leadership of the Reichsamtleiter Pg., Dr. Hörmann, whose tasks were: '1) Fighting all efforts and dangers connected with occultism. 2) Utilization of scientific research, positive observations and experiences for the purpose of cleansing of harmful frills in the area of occultism.' (Germ. Fed. Arch. NS 18/494, page 1, circular of Oct. 26, 1942) It follows from this document that occultism is only to be cleansed from 'harmful frills' and is not to be totally prohibited." [Stutterheim, 154 f.]

3  The statements of Himmler's astrologer, Wilhelm Wulff, on the engagement of a group of occultists for special tasks find confirmation with Hagen. Himmler, supposedly, established for it the "Operation Mars": "He had the earlier famous clairvoyants, astrologers, pendulum-interpreter, etc. gathered from all German concentration camps and 'ordered' them to find out Mussolini's location. Whoever was successful was promised freedom and one-hundred-thousand reichsmark. The 'occultists' of a certain name had, as is known, been arrested following Heydrich's orders, after the Führer's deputy, Rudolf Hess's flight to England, and taken to a concentration camp: Hess had been something of a protector of occult sciences and follower. Now, about forty of them were reactivated for the 'Operation Mars' and gathered into a working team at a firmly cordoned off villa at the Wannsee … The superintendent of this villa were the occultist were gathered, was very well known to me. The building served the Reichssicherheitshauptamt also as a hotel for special guests … On August 18, Himmler again visited his occult team at

Himmler did not only passively consult Wulff, he was, as Wulff writes, also familiar with the details of astrology: "In a few words Himmler explained to me his basic attitude towards astrology and its related areas. He spoke vividly and rather interestingly. His presentation displayed his good knowledge of this much reviled science ... He vividly reported several of his own experiences and his observations and experiences with certain positions of the moon ... saying that he started his own major actions always upon certain, little known moon constellations, which he was very familiar with. ..."[1] "He used expressions of astrological technique which he had not heard from me. He spoke of the Trigon-Aspect, the dual-body sign and the elevation of a planet."[2] Commenting on the prohibition of astrology in Germany, Himmler, according to Wulff, said: "We need strict astrology prohibition. Whoever violates this new decree must expect, should we catch him, to be locked up in a concentration camp until the war's end. We cannot permit others, beyond ourselves, to occupy themselves with astrology. Astrology must remain '*privilegium singulorum*' in the national-socialist state and is not for the mass of the people."[3] Shown here is the customary, hypocritical action vis-à-vis other occultists and gnostics. Not that the scene (Even the ariosophic guiding intellectual of racial fanaticism, Adolf Lanz, was hit with writing prohibition.[4]) is being fought because it is consid-

---

    Wannsee. A Berlin pendulum interpreter, equipped with the bright mind, typical for the city's residents, requested Himmler with enigmatic hints to follow him to his room. After various preparations that had to affect Himmler's psychic disposition inevitably, he began to have his pendulum swing over a map of Italy. And, lo and behold, the pendulum showed a clear swing between the islands of Corsica and Sardinia! Himmler was satisfied ... This is how momentous decision were arrived at in the Third Reich, at least occasionally. It is understood that this pendulum interpreter was, so to speak, in my service. I could have given him instructions through the superintendent to name the island Maddalena specifically, but I had refrained from it, since this all to precise accuracy could have caused suspicion, as credulous Himmler was about occult things. Of course, it must not be kept silent that this pendulum interpreter had other successes afterwards. Following Himmler's promise, he was truly set free, with his pendulum art used as a military-technical oddity of first grade for the finding of Allied ship convoys. Supposedly, as a leading officer of Großadmiral Dönitz's staff assured me convincingly, he made discoveries which matched the results of aerial reconnaissance exactly." [Hagen, 135 ff.]

1    Wulff, 153 f.
2    Wulff, 162
3    Wulff, 154
4    Daim, 22. – Stutterheim arrives at a similar view of the motives about the analysis result for the motive of a prohibition of diverse NS-predecessors with regard to the Thule

ered irrational, but because it is feared as competition. Astrologers could have predicted a poor war ending and instead of the Light-bringer Hitler, another charismatic Guru figure could have found the people's favor. Worse still was the danger of being mocked at home and abroad for occult practices. The public distancing was celebrated in just that exaggerated measure by which the true entanglement of several NS-Greats operated in these border areas. It thus is no surprise that Himmler, toward the end of the war when he met Norbert Masur, a representative of the Jewish World Congress, did not introduce Wulff as an astrologer. Wulff: "Of course, I was not introduced as Himmler's astrologer, but as 'Sanskrit researcher' – as it was called in Himmler's order."[1]

---

Organization: "The are many agreements between the program and the symbolics of the Thule Organization and the national-socialist movement, which is why Sebottendorf – failing to recognize the competitive situation – had hoped to gain honors in the 'Third Reich." [Stutterheim, 140]

1   Wulff, 207

# 7 The Paranoia: Baron Gotthard von der Osten-Sacken

In 1924, Baron Gotthard von der Osten-Sacken, an emigree from the Baltic, and retired Imperial-Russian Frigate-Captain, published a paper that could be called the memoirs of his previous stay in Germany.[1] There, peculiar things had happened to the Baron, so that he quickly – as was stated also in his book's title – that he thought to find himself – "in the power of dark forces." The entire presentation is so irrational that only original citations can provide a proper impression of the story and the mental condition of its author:

"By now, I have been in Berlin [at the beginning of the 20s] for more than two years, until the Jews and their accomplices found out how to make life there impossible for me and to drive me from Berlin. During the Kapp-Days, when the mood was most tense, I was walking around noon along the Kurfürtstendamm … A young Jew came towards me, clearly blocked my way in passing, and pushed me in a most hurtful manner." From his perspective, a visit to a bank proceeded also suspiciously: "When I returned for the second or third time, the representative of the stock division, a Jewish gentleman, asked me in a conspicious manner, this peculiar question: 'Do you wish to place your orders with our bank?' I said yes, but wondered about the question that clearly hinted that my patronage was not desired. This was another provocative behavior by a Jew without the least cause of mine."[2] "At this time, I believe it was August, I noticed for the first time instances that gave me reason to believe that I was observed on the street and even everywhere … I made the annoying observation that Jewish fellow-travelers [in the street car], of which there were, at the time, in Berlin already more than enough, made themselves at home in a not to be mistaken way opposite of me, even when there was no crowding and there was more than enough space. It could not be overlooked that a great number of Jews knew me by appearance. Today, their method of how to take aim at a person is well known to me. Obviously, the respective person is mentioned to a small circle of Jews, and every member of this circle takes care that all the members of another circle connected to his own, become acquainted with the appearance of the selected person. Then, every member of the new circle introduces a new, to

---

1   Essad Bey mentions a Baron von Osten-Sacken who, already about 1918 had supposedly lived for thirty years with his wife in Kisil-su (Turkmenistan). [Reiss, 63]
2   Osten-Sacken, 6

him answerable, circle, etc., etc., until the selected victim has become broadly known. I have no real proof of this assumption, only hints, that explain in this or a similar way how, in a big city like Berlin, in a certain part of town, in the course of a few weeks or months, it is possible to become unwillingly a well-known personality who one can, in a harmless way, declare war on in order to destroy the man's life ... The more I used the street cars, the more I noticed the intention to physically touch me. Wherever the opportunity presented itself to pass by me, it was used to softly brush against me, to touch me, to touch my overcoat, the brim of my hat, to brush against my advancing foot, and to give other such behavior free reign."[1] Osten-Sacken, therefore, leaves Berlin to travel to Dresden, where he is admitted to a hospital: "The manners of the people who carried me on the stretcher from the ambulance through the long garden of the Dresden Hospital were almost brutal. In one of the corridors, my arm was bumped against a door so hard that it hurt. I was admitted to a common hospital room and put to bed. Doctors were present, who questioned me. I spoke of the Jews. I was told that there were no Jews in this hospital. I knew better ... What kind of secret organization was this which tormented ill people? ... Who instructed these people? Of course, they were unaware who stood behind them. They had likely been told to be facing a questionable personality ... I knew who was behind. It was the Jew ... My brothers were called from Berlin, but I was unable to tell anyone anything. I would not have been understood ... One day a young man appeared in the door and called loudly into the room: 'Shaving desired?' – Shave a deathly ill man? Maybe the Jewish way? ... Some of the personnel and the caretakers displayed unsympathetic characteristics ... they looked at me penetratingly, silently, just as the Jews had last looked at me in Berlin."[2] After he was released, the machinations of "secret organizations, which spun their webs from a secret center to the farthest distances" supposedly continued. "What kind of odd things these were with ... the dead turkey in front of my window – the small suitcase on the stairs. Who put it there, the servant or the housemaid? Or was there still a third, secret force in the game that involuntarily played its devilish game by Jewish rules."[3] According to Osten-Sacken the devil also had its claws in the game of the secret organizations: "On this principle rests the devilish idea of a secret and criminal, foreign racial organization, served by many Christians and to which Christians fall victim. This devilish matter has

---

1 Osten-Sacken, 11
2 Osten-Sacken, 32 f.
3 Osten-Sacken, 55

not been invented for me, and I am not its first victim … May the Jews beware that the day will come, when it will be said and written with greater right: 'Entry to Jews forbidden.'"[1] "Whoever sows the wind will earn the storm."[2] After the Baron had been served in an unfriendly manner by a barber's employee, the Baron asked himself: "Are all barbers members of a miserable, nasty association of Jewish origin? Not all. I know one in Berlin … who … remained decent. I can refer to the man."[3] Von der Osten-Sacken continued to describe another imagined method of pursuit, he later claimed to have experienced in Munich: The whistling of the Jews: "Usually, the moment I enter the inner railroad area, there is more or less loud whistling … almost exactly as in Dresden and Königstein. I always use the train at 12 o'clock 18 minutes. The Jews know this very well … Evenings, when I go for dinner to Barerstraße, there is loud whistling and almost always, without exception, while I eat."[4] In Munich, too, he claims to have been touched in a street car: "I knew enough, the man was a 'toucher.'"[5] Freemasonry, too, was suspect to the Baron: "It appears to me that the number '2' plays an important role in Freemasonry … Twice, a little known person sitting by my bedside, checked my pulse in Dresden while I was seriously ill … I was asked twice in my business office whether a typewriter had been sold … Twice, my shoulder was touched by a previous Russian minister's assistant in the most noticeable manner … Twice, one of two Jews passing me on the street said the key words 'Cellar, Cellar.' Twice, always twice."[6]

But soon he said he learned what kind of game was being played against him. He had accidentally followed the conversation of two sailors: "These two gentlemen mentioned, even if only in passing, without giving names, someone who supposedly had been condemned to 'moral death.' 'Condemned to moral death!' Something like this is totally new to me. Never had I known that someone could be condemned to such a punishment. Like lightning I was struck by the inspiration. This fits me. I have often asked myself how to describe the method to which the Jews had obviously condemned me. 'Moral Death' – that must have been it. That was it! This explained everything!"[7] The Baron described the assumed, final consequence: "When the Jew cannot make a Christian ill himself,

---

1 Osten-Sacken, 114 f.
2 Osten-Sacken, 121
3 Osten-Sacken, 74
4 Osten-Sacken, 76 f.
5 Osten-Sacken, 80
6 Osten-Sacken, 98 f.
7 Osten-Sacken, 72

a serving Christian must take care to present the condemned Christian as ill, as abnormal, as insane, sufficiently sick for admittance to an asylum ... I can refer to the person who recently told me: 'It has been said that you are insane.' ... Should my 'enemy' of late express some final interest about my health condition? He applied the method of touch for a long time, and with great eagerness, but seemingly not intensely enough."[1]

Even the psychologically untrained lay person would have no difficulty observing, in the light of the irrational portrayals, that the Baron was obviously in urgent need of psychological help – for acute paranoia. At best, one would put the book aside – if one would even read it to its end – or leave it be with a smile, or if engaged, would get the author expert help via his publisher, or – and this is the most likely case – describe the book as a poor purchase and entrusting it to the waste basket. Not so Himmler. Already in the year of its publishing in 1924, he read it and commented on this reading experience as follows: "Description of the Jewish system of condemnation to Moral Death. It is possible that, caused by it, a certain persecution complex enters. However, the system exists without doubt and is perpetrated by Jews."[2] Mind you: According to Himmler, the persecution complex does not presuppose the author's point of view of the world, but that the 'Jewish System' existed in reality and consequently – quasi as proof of the effectiveness of this system – von der Sacken had fallen ill. The System had made him insane. At this point, the question about Himmler's psychic health must be raised.

---

1   Osten-Sacken, 94
2   Himmler, Reading list, title 221, transcription page 32

Otto Rahn's „Hotel Restaurant des Marroniers" in the South of France (Ussat-les-Bains), 2004 abandoned (photo: Wegener)

# 8 The Polars: Maurice Magre, Jean-Marqués-Rivière, Gaston de Mengel

In 1933 the writer Otto Rahn published his well regarded book "Crusade against the Grail," in which he summarized the results of his journey to France[1] in the year 1930. Rahn was a SS-man since 1936.[2] In March of 1939, Rahn, who, in the meantime had risen to SS-Obersturmführer, chose suicide – likely because his homosexual orientation was incompatible with SS-guidelines.[3] In southwest France Rahn searched for the secret treasure of the Katharers, the Grail. In 1244, before Castle Montségur, the spiritual center of these Middle Age gnostics, was stormed by representatives of the Inquisition together with the French King, some Katharers supposedly had escaped from the besieged castle. In their hands: the Grail. Maurice Magre, from Toulouse, who inspired Rahn,[4] fabulated already: "Later, four knights came ... to the fortress of Montségur; under their coats they hid the legacy of Joseph of Arimathia, the emerald in the shape of a lily, containing Christ's blood ..."[5]

The idea of immortality[6] is also carried by the Christian cultural horizon in the myth of the Holy Grail, the chalice Christ supposedly used for the last supper and in which, later, upon his crucifixion, his blood was supposedly captured. Joseph of Arimathia is thought to have brought it later to England. Lately, following the highly popular Hollywood flick "Indiana Jones and the last Crusade," it is generally granted that the miraculous force was able to confer eternal life. The image of the Grail symbolizes therefore, in an idealized way, the search for immortality. And it cannot be excluded that Spielberg's script writers were inspired by Otto Rahn's life. A filming of the "Crusade against the Grail"

---

1   Lange, Rahn, 33
2   Lange, Rahn, 61
3   Otto Rahn, SS-Obersturmführer since Sept. 11, 1938, died March, 17, 1939 acc. to Meyer, S. 266, ser. no. 6380, department RFSS Staff and correcting notebook, page 31. Even in 1941 Himmler remembered Rahn. [manual entry Himmler's in his service calendar on March 17, 1941: "17:00 Vogelsang – Remembering Otto Rahn." [Himmler, Dienstkalender, 133]
4   Lange, Rahn, 31
5   Quoting Lange, Rahn, 234 f. – Magre, Maurice: Smaragdfeuer oder die Liebe des Narren – Märchenroman einer Graleinweihung in den Pyrenäen, Bad Münstereifel 1986
6   Comment to some opinions Himmler's to the question of immortality: Ackermann, 68 ff.

in 1934 by "a German movie company (the largest)" had once been thought to have been written according to Rahn's statements.¹

For all that, the treasure, if it ever existed is, historically, rather trivial money, since the Middle Age sources speak only of *pecunia* – there is no word of any chalice.² Himmler, more specifically: his spiritual mentor, a former patient in a psychiatric clinic, Karl-Maria Wiligut, aka Weisthor, became aware of Rahn by way of the "Crusade,"³ so that Rahn's journey to France in his search of the Grail, was not supported by Himmler, even when Rahn, a year after publication, wrote to a good friend: "High-ranking colleagues will support us: first of all, Baron Evola, Italy's most influential fascist writer, and one of the closest staff-members of Mussolini's. We have allies in Germany, in Switzerland and Holland, as well as in France, whom one can by no means call 'just someone' ..."⁴ Himmler's later sponsorship of the young author confirms, in any case, a far-reaching sympathy for Rahn's concern. Supposed SS-expeditions to Montségur or an overflight of the *pog* by army aircraft at the time of the summer solstice belong, however, in the realm of fantasy. Other motives for a grail search by Himmler lies closer: Himmler had a female ancestor, who had been burned in 1629 as a witch, whom he may have assumed had been burned as a sympathizer of the German Katharers.⁵ Leading NS-ideologist Rosenberg saw in the Katharers the remains of the Visigothic migration and stylized their death into a kind of race martyrism. In the 40s, this idea may also have driven Himmler to Rosenberg's support, particularly since this core idea of a unison of faith with the Germanic-Visigoth race, with reference to Bogumilen/Katharer-grave stones in Croatia, was discussed anew – now by the SS.⁶

Somewhere in Berlin, two men met in 1937.⁷ One was named Heinrich Himmler and was at this time the second-most powerful man in the state after

---

1 Lange, Rahn, 11, 152 f.
2 Lange, Rahn, 236
3 Lange, Rahn, 56 f.
4 Lange, Rahn, 154
5 Wegener, Kelten, 77
6 Wegener, Schuler, 64 ff.
7 In a letter dated March 9, 1937 the personal staff of SS-Reichsführer, Brigadeführer Wiligut advised: "The SS-Reichsführer consents to several discussions of Mr. de Mengel in your house. He may yet wish to briefly visit with Mr. de Mengel." [Germ. Fed. Arch., NS19-3974, page 5] And Lachner informed Wolff on May 4, 1937 in a letter: "I have expressed to him [De Mengel], that the SS-Reichsführer has read his work, as far as he has been able to access it, with interest and would have liked to speak with Mr. de Mengel once more. However, because of the SS-Reichsführer's present heavy work load

Hitler. With his SS, Himmler had established a kind of alternative army which, with its hundreds of thousands of men, not only represented a decisive defensive and political power in the state[1] but could make ideological opponents disappear at any time in concentration camps. For a year, Himmler was simultaneously head of the German police, a more domestic power. As "Reichskommissar for the Strengthening of German Traditions" (RFK), he was shortly to initiate one of the greatest migrations in Europe. This migration eventually ended in a catastrophe as had never occurred before.

We know nothing about the two men's meeting place; it may have been a small street café. The origin of the second man speaks for such a place: The more than 60 year old[2] private scholar,[3] Gaston de Mengel, came directly from Paris. On the whole, this Briton was a rather mysterious character.[4] His first

---

it has been not possible as much as he would have liked." [Germ. Fed. Arch., NS19-3974, page 30]

1. Wegner [sic], 80, 210. In January of 1929, SS-membership was about 280. By the end of 1933 it had risen to 209,014. By 1943/44 the Waffen-SS had about half a million soldiers.
2. Germ.Fed.Arch, NS19-3974, page 47, Letter dated Aug. 19, 1937 Schlarb to SS-Untersturmführer Ruppmann: "Furthermore, it must be considered that he [de Mengel] is over 60 years old and therefore tends toward one-sidedness."
3. Karl-Maria Wiligut called De Mengel in a letter dated Febr. 19, 1937 a "private scholar" [Barch, NS19-3974, page 2]. Frenzolf Schmid writes of "Professor DE MENGEL" [Barch, NS19-3974, page 8, Letter of March 21, 1937 of SS-Sturmbannführer Schmid to von Lachner]. This designation is not found with anyone else.
4. For de Mengel's activities one may consider an explanation which must remain, however, very much speculative: The French occultist, Anne Osmont, wrote 1941 in her memoirs that René Guénon who was next to Papus the best known French occultist, had brutally opened her eyes about the Theosophes. Osmont: "I sometimes asked myself why such respected speakers came from afar to convert us, especially from Anglo-Saxon countries. If we, as Guénon assured us, were only a division of the secret service, their goal becomes obvious and I must no longer ask myself who assumed the expenses for personnel and the organization. I am not speaking about the lecturers; they are rich, something I know only too well." [Osmont, 56] De Mengel was a British citizen. [Lachner letter to the head of the personal staff of SS-Gruppenführer Wolff of May 14, 1937: "Mr. de Mengel advises via Ms. Schlarb that he inquired at the British Consulate in Berlin (he is a British citizen) about the travel formalities for his intended trip to Helsinki." [Germ. Fed. Arch, NS19-3974, page 37 f.] The only bow expressly mentioned citizenship shows that it was as yet obviously unknown during de Mengel's stay in Berlin and his conversation with Himmler. Claims concerning supposed secret service activities of comrades-in-arms and competitors were, however, no rarity in the occult milieu of the time. Mail Wegener-ITT from 02/09/2011 via ITT.com-contact form: "Subject: Your archives: Search for Gaston de Mengel 1967. Dear ladies and gentlemen, I'm a german historian in search

bibliographically-accessible article was published in 1913. It was about the transmutation (usually meant to be the conversion of simple metals into gold or silver). In the journal of the London Alchemist Society, its author was named as: "Gaston de Mengel." In 1925/1926 his name is spelled "Gaston Demengel" in the journal *"Penser et Agir."* In 1928-1930, his articles in *"Voile d'Isis"* are subsequently signed with Gaston de Mengel. In 1931, an article about Atlantis is found in the same journal under the name "Gaston de Mangel," as well as an article about the aspects of the Hindu term "Shakti," once again showing "Gaston de Mengel" as the author. Then, an article on "The Unfaithfulness of the Freemasons" appears in 1935 in *"Mercure de France"*[1] under the pseudonym "Inturbidus" [Latin for quiet]. Since the first name seems to be the most probable, and "de Mangel" likely is a typing error, the name "Gaston de Mengel" is subsequently used. De Mengel's baggage held parts of his previous life's work: Dozens of articles and lectures about a highly explosive subject. No, it did not deal with secret documents on the French military or design plans for building of new, pioneering fighter aircraft. It dealt with such illustrious subjects as Indian healing techniques, the question about the esoteric of music, or "just" the Middle Age Templar Knights.

Doubtlessly, the conversation proceeded to the satisfaction of both, Himmler and de Mengel, since there were further conversations with subordinate assistants of Himmler's that at last lead to the occultist's texts to be copied by the SS and then stored in a safe on Kaspar-They street 33.[2] What kind of papers were these?

CONTENTS. Like Himmler, de Mengel was occupied with the search for Atlantis (1931). I have already addressed this aspect of de Mengel's work in

---

    for the descendants of Gaston Pakenham de Mengel, London, who assigns patents to ITT in 1946 and 1967 (see http://www.freepatentsonline.com/2562894.pdf and http://www.freepatentsonline.com/3303375.pdf ). It would be possible, that the inventor Mr. de Mengel is the same british man who met german SS-Leader Heinrich Himmler in 1937. Any information about de Mengel's vita, especially his London address in 1967 would help. Thank you very much, Franz Wegener, historian M.A." – Regrettably, I have received no reply from ITT (March, 22, 2013). ITT-employees are claimed to have connections with the CIA and British intelligence service. [Article: "ITT: Weltkonzern zwischen Politik und Profit," in: Der Spiegel, 27/1973, online presently under http://www.spiegel.de/spiegel/print/d-41986615.html ]

1    *"Mercure de France"* [1890-1965] was the leading French magazine of Symbolism – an art form upon also Stefan George built. [Webb, Underground, 175]

2    German Fed. Archives (BArch), NS 19/3974, page 1

the new edition of "The Atlantis World View" (2003)¹ De Mengel's article on the traditional elements of gnosticism likely intrigued Himmler because of his interest in the Katharers, as it did Otto Rahn, who was the interpreter during de Mengel's stay in Berlin. In his article *"Les élements traditionnels dans le Gnosticism,"* de Mengel falls back on secondary German-language literature (Wilhelm Anz: To the Question on the Origin of Gnosticism, Leipzig 1897; Hans Waitz: Simon Magus, in ancient Christian literature; Harnack: History of Dogmata, I). A literature listing by M. Clavelle is attached to the article which, first of all, reflects the French-language gnostic literature from the middle to the end of the 19th century.² De Mengel addresses also the gnostic anti-Jewish stance, when he asks himself why the gnostics place the World builder, the Demiurg, so far down in their cosmogony. Doubtlessly, because the gnostics felt such a deep revulsion for the God of the Jews, who, in the Old Testament, appeared to them so violent, vengeful and stupid, although He was supposed to be the actual creator of the world, so that they, more or less consciously caricatured him in the form of their Demiurg.³ But he does not forget to mention that it is certain that the Jewish secret teachings, the "Cabbala",⁴ influenced the gnostic systems, foremost that of Marcus.⁵

Also, I wish to mention as more detailed three subjects representative of other publications of de Mengel, in order to provide insight into the thematic world of the French esoteric scene of the 20s. De Mengel's first article occupies

---

1  Wegener, AWB, 2. Edition, 29 ff.
2  Mengel, Gnosticisme, 691 ff.
3  Mengel, Gnosticisme, 695
4  Scholem about the Kabbala: "The Kabbala – literally: Tradition, that is esoteric tradition – is a movement in which, mainly between the 12th to 17th century the mystic tendencies of Judaism found ... their religious expression ... in multiple branchings. There is nothing like 'a doctrine of Kabbalists' ... In southern France, fed by covert, most likely Oriental sources, it saw its first light, in the same areas and time that saw in the non-Jewish surroundings the height of katharic or new-Manichaean movement. In the Spain of the 13th century, it grew in a rapid, surprisingly intense development to its fully developed forms, with its height expressed in the pseudo-epigraphic book Sohar of Rabbi Moses de Leon, which became a kind of bible of the Kabbalists ..." [Scholem, Gershom: "Zur Kabbala und ihrer Symbolik," Frankfurt/M. 1998, 7; citing Stutterheim, 49]
5  Mengel, Gnosticisme, 699. – Micha Brumlik: "It is historically no accident that anti-Judaism and anti-Semitism are, as of today, still feed on gnostic thought. This does not change anything of the fact that Gnosis probably arose in the fold of Jewish sects and that in Judaism itself, in Kabbala and Chassidism, gnostic tendencies take on a substantial space." [Brumlik, 20]

itself with the question of human immortality. A second article revolves around a special term of Hinduism: "Shakti." The third article addresses Freemasonry.

IMMORTALITY. In 1933 an article of de Mengel's appeared not in a French, but an international publication: The article's title was "Knowledge and Immortality," which appeared in the "Review of Philosophy and Religion," a publication giving Poona as its place of origin. In this article de Mengel discusses the relationships between reality accessible by consciousness, and the reality removed from mental perception. Then, by referencing the gnostic-platonic teachings, he discusses the question of possible human immortality.[1]

To approach this subject would require knowledge, and, in the final consequence, it would possibly be about – supra-human knowledge[2] – the existence of which could no longer be denied. Together with Alfred Binet (and Kant/Descartes) he points out that we reach conclusions from visual observations of moving objects on the abstract scheme of movement. Only the object is claimed to be visible, yet contained in it was movement as an idea.[3] Perception was taken from consciousness, behind which hid the Self as principle. This Self, this subject, was now [as a data-processing rule complex] necessarily thought to be nonphysical, without being spiritual immaterial.[4] At that, modern physiology would become stuck where insights on the perceptive apparatus ended: Lastly, electo-chemical changes in the eyes would transmit the signals from the outside world to the nerve center to there producing a *"mental impression"* of what was seen. Upon the question what would then happen, modern physiology was supposedly incapable of providing an answer. Disappointed by contemporary cognition science, de Mengel turned to the classic concepts, at first Aristotle's. Everything existing was thought to consist of a mix of two principles: That of Substance, or Matter, called *materia*, and that of Essence, called *forma*. De Mengel compares the influence of Essence on Matter with the influence of an invisible magnetic field. When the Essence of the perceived object would now, by means of the perceptive apparatus, strike the Essence of the Self, the *anima*, a copy of the object's Essence was there activated. It remained to understand that the general character of mental perception consisted in that we could receive the Essence of the perceived objects, but without getting in touch with the Matter, just like

---

1 Mengel, Knowledge, 33
2 Mengel, Knowledge, 34
3 Mengel, Knowledge, 35
4 Mengel, Knowledge, 39

wax could receive the impression of a seal without itself being of iron or gold. De Mengel refers also to the Yoga teachings of Bhikshu, wherein it is said that the objects of knowledge, although themselves inactive (themselves not producing wisdom), could nevertheless attract the always changing souls (*chittas*) and modify them according to their respective Essence.

De Mengel is calling strongly on Aristotelean philosophy. The elaboration of Matter by Essence, that is all creation, is, according to Aristotle, implemented on the basis of four principles:

1) the *causa materialis*. Everything originates from something, which is Matter.

2) the *causa formalis*. Everything originates into something, that is to a form, as quartz sand becomes a shaped glass.

3) the *causa finalis*. Everything originates because of something, that is for a specific purpose – in the case of the glass to drink from it.

4) the *causa movens*. Everything originates through something. The transition from its mere potential into reality (Entelechy, because it carries in it purpose, Telon) takes place through a moving cause, the principle of movement. – Glass will come into being from sand only in a moving process.

For Aristotle the world consists of matter. Matter is the essence of godhood. Next to Matter and Essence as the basic principles of this process, a third principle is added, that of Privation. Such as Brightness cannot be thought of without Darkness. Besides Matter as the basis and essence as the goal exists therefore at the beginning of the formation process the Not-yet-being, the negation of the coming form: its relative Not-being.

But all movement presupposes something that moves. For Aristotle this is the godhead. But since this godhead is a purely spiritual image, it cannot have any direct access on matter. And since the godhead is imagined as being absolute, it cannot move something poorly by itself, since it then – following the assumption that everything moving presupposed something moving – would not be absolute, i.e. independent of movement originating from it. How then, in the case of the godhead necessarily imagined unmoved can it move something? An approach at explanation is an analogy from the world of human relations. An attractive person awakens in his vis-à-vis a certain desire to approach him (repeated here is in principle the image of the magnet de Mengel used for the presentation of the Yoga teachings). The desiring person has this effect on his vis-à-vis even when not knowing his vis-à-vis, has no relationship with him, and does not even intend to make any move towards his vis-à-vis. He himself does not act[1] – does not move – yet his vis-à-vis does – in this example, possibly in the direction of a table. Just like the attractive person moves his vis-à-vis without moving, so the godhead moves as a nonmoving mover the world, without itself being a link in the chain of movements: "There is also something that moves ... which, although it is not moved, moves something else, something that is eternal, an entity and a realization. In this way the desired and the imagined moves; it moves, although it is not moved."[2] At another place it says: "... this [striving] is the matter, which, just like femaleness (desire) for maleness and ugliness for beauty."[3]

For Aristotle the heavenly bodies consists of an entity, the Ether, differing from the four elements. The idea of the Ether is founded on the observation that fire and air always orient themselves upward, but water and earth always downward. If a planet consisted of one of these four elements, it would need to move either upward or downward. A circular movement – as observed – would thus not be possible. Accordingly, there must be a *quinta essentia*, to which no matter is admixed, since, otherwise, the planet would sooner or later tire in its movement.[4]

Next to Aristotle de Mengel relied extensively on Plato.[5] Thus a triangle of paper and a triangle of wood, as well as a triangle engraved on a copper ball, would have something generally matching, being independent from the individual note of the object: the nature of the triangle – a surface, bordered by three lines. This nature is thought to be the idea of the triangle, its Idea.[6] Supposedly, the paper triangle is merely the expression in concrete terms of a copy of the principal essence, the archetypical idea of a triangle. We could recognize the caricature of a painting as such only, if we knew its original. We would not be able by force of abstraction and generalization to conclude from the execution on the underlying model, the concept, and since we were missing the standard of comparison, we could never realize that one of the copies would be without

---

1   See also Aristotle, Physik, VIII, 2, 253a
2   Aristotle, Metaphysik, XII, 7, 1072a
3   Aristotle, Physik, I, 9, 192a
4   Behler, 51 f.
5   Mengel, Knowledge, 48
6   Mengel, Knowledge, 44

errors. Therefore, this idea had to be already innate before we would come across a triangle. To imply something else would mean to succumb to the logical mistake of *petitio principii*.

At this point it is suggested that one take a short look at Plato's Idea theory. In contrast to Aristotle, Plato knows a creator, the Demiurg: However, this laborer produced from that which exists is not identical to God. He builds by the example of the only mentally perceivable, that is the "intelligible" world of ideas. These ideas must really exist, since they influence our actions as true causes, and because they can be thought as [conceivable things = existing things]. The intermediary in this world view is the soul. On the one hand it is tied to the material, on the other it communicates with ideas. Accordingly, it is the medium by which ideas can engage in the mentally conceivable world.[1] The creation of the world by the Demiurg by the example of Ideas is described in "Timaios": "... it, [the cosmos] needing to be considered, after the respective example [paradigm] by which its supervisor built it ... Thus created [the world] is built by the reflection and that which can be perceived by reason as well as the unchanged [the ideas]; but since this is so, it is necessary that this world is a copy of something."[2]

De Mengel now concluded that the images of the archetypes – would be images imprinted on the universal intellect (the Buddhi of Hindus, the Neshamah of the Hebrews, or the Greek Nous) – which, by the mediation of this very intellect were reproduced in the form of the received subject. The universal intellect stimulates by the allocation of concepts the Subjective Self.[3] Every human being ("possibly" with the exception of the feeble-minded[4]) has a certain contact with the universal intellect. The Subject, seeing e.g. a rose, is thought to assume the individual form of this rose, recognizing in it the idea of the flower, then grasping its beauty. One and the same person was thus grasping the special precept (the perceived image), the general concept and the transcendental. In order to adequately comprehend the Universal, consciousness itself would need to be universal. All being would therefore be nothing more than the realization of a reflection of the principal essence, whereby the individual essences of the existing would be more or less substantial parts of the principal essence. Unfor-

---

1 Dörrie, column 896 ff.
2 Plato, Timaios, 28b, in: Grassi, Vol. 5, 154 f.
3 Mengel, Knowledge, 49
4 A reminder to Du Prel's above cited statement that the "Insane" is proof for the existence of a higher consciousness, since he can act quite rational under hypnosis.

tunately, the sight of consciousness is veiled too densely to be in the position to differentiate between the individual forms into which it has entered, and its origin, the beam of principal essence, representing the real subject. Only a few had reached the point where they were able to differentiate between the self and the Self. Superhuman knowledge could therefore not be accessed by studies, but only through intuition. For explanation, de Mengel cited Dionysus Pseudo-Areopagita: "Only those know something about it who have attained a degree of higher knowledge. Among us are people with such a mind, appointed by such a favor, as far as it is possible for a human being to make himself resemble an angel. They are those who, by terminating all mental activities achieve unity with the indescribable light." This, supposedly, was Samadhi, for which the souls of Hindus thirsted.[1] Whoever had achieved it, would become a Yogi, having achieved unity. By cessation of his individuality he is saved from rebirths, his "self" has disappeared in favor of the Self. It was now united with all who had been saved by their identification of their self with the origin. I have attained the only true immortality. And he cites Johannes Baptista Van Helmont, who supposedly wrote in 1667 in *"Hortus Medicinae"*: "A magical force, deadened by sin, is latently asleep in man. It can be awakened by the grace of God or by the arts of the Cabbala. We can find in ourselves the pure and sacred knowledge if we succeed in separating ourselves from all external influences and letting us be guided by the inner light. At this level of concentration ... the mind ... can even reach God."[2] De Mengel refers to the historical development of the ecclesiastical teaching in matters of immortality, which did not provide for a by Nature immortal soul, but made immortality dependent on the grace of God. Inevitably, de Mengel sees this totally different from his gnostic perspective and points even to angels of human origin in the Asian tradition. Even Saint Thomas admitted that angels were a mixture of matter and essence *('Et ideo positio illa videtur verior esse, scilicet quod in angelo est compositio ex materia et forma.')* De Mengel: "If we be anathema, at least we are in goodly company."[3] For the record: According to de Mengel the question of immortality is a question of personal, spiritual cognition. Once this has been realized, man changes into a superhuman, immortal being: An angel.[4]

---

1  Mengel, Knowledge, 55
2  Mengel, Knowledge, 56
3  Mengel, Knowledge, 61
4  A short text compilation sent to Himmler via the Ahnenerbe summarized these theses wrongly as follows: "[The treatise] also explains briefly the different modalities of human progress after his earthly death." [Germ. Fed. Arch., NS19-3974, page 19]

SHAKTI. In 1931, there appeared in the French esoteric publication *"Voile d'Isis,"* – "Veil of Isis," a multipart article of de Mengel's about a central concept of the Hindu doctrine: Shakti." De Mengel explains that the term "shakti" means strength. He pointed out that the term has many connections and similarities to the Hebrew term "Shekinah." De Mengel connects "Shakti" with the "radiant bliss", Anananda, of Hinduism which, simultaneously was to be the Hebrew "Binah," Cabbalists called the "Highest Mother," Gnostics "Our Lady of the Holy Spirit,"[1] and Tantrics would call "The Great Mother."[2] He also discovers in the Hindu doctrine the basics of the Aristotelean Form doctrine: "One can see that Purusha and Prakriti are the two poles of the manifesting activity that form the productive creativity; the first provides the essence, the second the substance and both principles together constitute everything existing ... in the existing bodies the essence becomes *forma* ... the substance *materia*." This *materia* is however not to be mistaken for the second matter, which is nothing else but the Ether. De Mengel assigns to the duality of essence and substance – analogous to the Indian Sanskrit designation of the terms – the duality of male-female. This is why – opposite to common opinion – the female is out for realization, while the male occupies himself with concepts. Shakti is thought to be the realizing substance, synonymous with the Prakriti, a divine mother, mother of gods and humans, mother of the universe, weighed equally to Ishtar with the Chaldeans, Isis with the Egyptians, and the holy virgin with Christians.[3] He also connects Shakti with the Kundalini, the sexual energy of the tantric Yoga. The Shakti is thought to rise [in the body] over the Chakras, the centers of the soul, standing in relationship to the Tattvas Ap (water), Tejas (fire), Vâyu (air), Akâsha, (ether) and Manas (mentality/reason).[4]

---

1   James Webb sees especially two Heretic Groups being in touch with the sources of occult tradition: The Katharer and the libertine Heretics of Free Spirit in the 13th/14th century, who said about themselves that they were God - and could therefor not sin: "The heresy of the Free Spirit might also be described as a form of Gnosticism, this time the libertine variety. It seems to have had connections with a new school of Neo-Platonic mysticism represented by Meister Eckhart (1260-1327) whose thought was in his own lifetime condemned by the papacy as heretical in a series of twenty-eight articles ... Whether the influence of the sort of Neo-Platonism which Eckhart professed had any influence on the cult or not ... there is no doubt that the heresy was effectively Gnostic." [Webb, Underground, 207 f.]
2   Mengel, Shakti, 733
3   Mengel, Shakti, 736 f.
4   Mengel, Shakti, 749. – De Mengel liked to cite here from the tantric texts of Arthur Avalon: "The Serpent Powers", Madras 1924; "Principles of Tantra", London, 1914 and

With this text de Mengel continued with his usual comparative interpretation approach. As usual, European theologies are compared with Asian and Near-Eastern findings, in order to underline, in the final consequence, the similar bases of the optically so very different religions. With this he follows a theosophic approach which Blavatsky had already pursued in her writings – always searching for an "Urreligion," for what appears to be similar today, may have once had a common departure point.

FREEMASONRY. In 1935 de Mengel commented in *"Mercure de France"* about the "Unfaithfulness of the Freemasons." This is the last known publication before his meeting with Himmler. Freemasonry is a subject in which Himmler is thought to have been highly interested. This is confirmed by his reading list wherein numerous books about Freemasonry and their supposed conspiracies are listed.[1] Himmler's interest was not restricted to the German-language area,

---

Mahânirvâna Tantra, London 1913. [De Mengel, Shakti, 754] De Mengel's article in "Voile d'Isis" is followed, by the way, by a paper *"Le Grand-Oevre alchimique d'après une ècole musulmane"* which refers to Rudolf von Sebottendorf's "Die Praxis der alten türkischen Freimaurerei, der Schlüssel zum Verständnis der Alchimie," Leipzig 1924. The author points out that he received the text from Paul Chacornac and that Sebottendorf was the former editor of the Astrologischen Rundschau. – Stutterheim writes about Sebottendorf: "The Secret society of Thule was founded in Munich in 1918 as a branch of the Germanenorden. Of great influence, and especially of great popularity, was in this case the con man and adventurer, Rudolf Glauer, from Hoyerswerda, who called himself 'von Sebottendorf' and invented for this name an exciting biography." [Stutterheim, 118; Olenhusen, Albrecht Götz von et al., article: "Der Germanenorden 1912-1922," in: Jacob, 195ff.]

1  Books referencing Freemasonry in Himmler's reading list: Schwartz-Bostunitsch, Gregor: "Freimaurerbuch" (borrowed from Frenzolf Schmid); Wichtl, Friedrich: "Weltfreimaurerei, Weltrevolution, Weltrepublik – Eine Untersuchung über Ursprung und Endziele des Weltkriegs" ["World-Freemasonary, World-Revolution, World-Republic – An examination of the origin and final goals of the World War"]; Himmler: "A book that explains everything and tells us against whom we need to fight first"; Daiber, Albert Ludwig: "Elf Jahre Freimaurer"; Bolanden, Conrad v.: "Der Teufel in der Schule" and the same: "Die Sünde wider den heiligen Geist"; Molo, W. von: "Ein Deutscher ohne Deutschland – Ein Friedrich List-Roman" [Himmler, Reading list]. On the subject Nationalsocialism and Freemasonry: Neuberger, Helmut: "Winkelmaß und Hakenkreuz – Die Freimaurer und das Dritte Reich", Munich 2001; the about 80,000 volumes from the inventory of lodge libraries confiscated by the SS between 1933 and 1936 in the Deutsche Reich today are stored in the Masonica collection of the university library Poznań/Posen, for research via German Federal Archives, Finder book BarchAStF/M, Fsg.2/1-F, Finder book, S.V f. (Microfiche catalog)) see also: Lorenz, 49

but, following the occupation, reached also by means of his secret services into France.

De Mengel mentions in his article, political and other misdeeds of the Freemasons that supposedly caused a general uproar against them.[1] Another subject of the article is about the initiations: "One can see that the term 'Initiation' [dedication] can be used in another context than is today customary in the West. With reference to its meaning, the way we use it, as it was used in ancient times in Europe and is today still in the Orient, we have not found a better definition than Madame Alexandra David-Neel's[2] given in her book *'Initiations Lamaïques'*: She says, that the principle idea we connect with 'initiation,' is the revelation of a secret teaching, the admission to learn particular mysteries, while *angkour* (the Tibetan term translated to Initiation), means first of all the transmission of a physical force, a power ... Accordingly, the initiated person must not necessarily be in the know or be a saint, but he can even be completely feeble-minded or a rogue." Meanwhile, it was said that Freemasonry had gotten off the proper path. As a cure de Mengel discussed the possibility, following the elimination of 70-80% of undesired and unsuitable lodge members (he claimed to have received this number from high-ranking members of Freemasonry) to found a new hermetic organization from the remainder of the Masons. But from where should one take the initiation for this organization? This initiation could only be conferred by Freemasons, who, at the same time, would still be something else and be in an orthodox initiation chain. Or would it be necessary for the members of the new organization to accept receiving the initiation from insiders, who are not Freemasons (these could be found).[3] To destroy Freemasonry – if this is not an unworkable task – would mean, on the one hand, to point out the incomprehension with respect to the ploy of clandestine groups dwelling in the heart of Masonry, who stood behind it, who had worked for generations on the demise of the organization, and for whom those that had diverged from the Masonry's path of virtue – as had Judaism – were nothing else but instruments. On the other hand, de Mengel also addresses the question of whether Freemasonry might not be a clandestine Jewish establishment, or had at least been infiltrated by Jews: "Many people believe that Freemasonry is a creation of Judaism. The reality looks different. The use of Jewish terms in the Masonry ritual does not necessarily indicate a Jewish

---

1    Mengel, Infidelité, 310
2    Alexandra David-Neel: a Paris-born 1868 Tibet researcher (+1969)
3    Mengel, Infidelité, 322

connection. One could say just as easily that the Christian ritual, consisting in large part of the recitation of Jewish texts, confirms a Jewish infiltration of Christianity. The speculative Freemasonry that arose in 1717, follows without a doubt Protestant inspiration; if Jews, clearly later, got mixed up in it, than they did it in the way the Rosenkreuzer groups did in earlier times, either in their own interest or by the instigation of occult groups of which we have hinted already. The existence of these groups is known only to a very small number of individuals ... among those (individuals) is René Guénon, best known for his writings confirming a rarely to be found understanding of the Hindu teachings. In his work 'The Theosophy – History of a Pseudo-Religion,' this author relates to us by means of the subject of the false redeemer, the role of hidden groups: 'The differences [of the diverse esoteric groups], as far as their not being very superficial, are in all cases clearly less fundamental than their common tendencies; and one can say about it, that all ... is done for the realization of a singular plan[1] ... Beyond this we do not believe that the Theosophes nor the Occultists or the Spiritualists will have the power to resolve such a task successfully and completely on their own; but could they hide behind all these movements a terrible thing which may not even be known by their leaders and to which they are nevertheless nothing but mere instruments?'" De Mengel continues: "We cannot repeat it often enough: The speculative Freemasonry like Judaism and like Theosophy, of which René Guénon reports, and – to add – like the political movements, national and global, be they ever so contradictory, they are all nothing but instruments, manipulated by groups equipped with a power, all of them aiming for a singular and terrible goal ... In every respect a straightening out of Freemasonry in the sense of tradition would therefore be better."[2] But he did not want to deny that, considering what had already happened, such a correction would probably remain a utopia. In contrast to all other available articles of de Mengel's, this article is signed with the pseudonym "Inturbidus" (Latin for quiet). Might de Mengel have told Himmler of his assumptions? This is likely, given that this article about the "secret organizations" was prepared two years later for the SS.[3] – De Mengel's conspiracy theories probably found an open ear with Himmler, since he obviously had pronounced paranoid traits,

---

1   Reading tip to the "Plan": Eco, Umberto: "Das Foucaultsche Pendel," Munich 1992 ;-)
2   Mengel, Infidelité, 323 f.. In volume 1-VII-1935, pages 53-66 of *"Mercure de France"* is found a discussion of racism and the Führer principle in Germany under the title *"Considérations inactuelles sur le racisme"* by Kadmi Cohen.
3   A report, unfortunately not available.

as his positive evaluation of the paranoid expositions of von Osten-Sacken's, illustrated before, confirm.

De Mengel's text was also reviewed by the no. 2 of French Occultism, René Guénon (1886-1951), to whom de Mengel referred at times in the article. De Mengel's pseudonym, "Inturbidus" was not resolved by Guénon and the content of de Mengel's article about Freemasonry was critiqued only weakly, by saying that the information taken from one of de Mengel's sources were not the most certain. Guénon sees also the intention by "Inturbidus" to establish an alternative order to Freemasonry, but views it skeptically: If the new organization is not to have any connection with the old Freemasonry, why should it then not recruit its members among the Freemasons, instead of from a totally different milieu? Only a change in the Freemasons' mentality would help.[1]

This should serve as examples of de Mengel's contents, as far as they are reflected in his writings.

How did de Mengel get to Berlin? He had been invited by Yrjö von Grönhagen. On February 19, 1937 the SS-Brigade Leader K. M. Wiligut wrote to SS-Group-Leader Wolff of the personal staff of the SS-Reichsführer: "I wish to report immediately on the discussions [with Mr. de Mengel and Mr. von Grönhagen] on Nov. 16 and Nov. 18, 1937. As is known by the SS-Reichsführer through Mr. von Grönhagen, Mr. de Mengel is presently staying in Berlin. Following the suggestion and arrangement of Mr. v. Grönhagen, two discussions took place giving a brief overview of his research studies, and further intentions. According to his own as well as Mr. v. Grönhagen's statements, he has at his disposal an exceptionally broad span of literature, rare of its kind. Mr. de Mengel showed me some of these works. His studies cover pre-Christian, Indian, Persian and, in part, Chinese literature, addressing the development of different spiritual and religious questions; among others, he is interested in the Edda, the Vedas, the Cabala, etc. Special studies deal with calculations of the building of pyramids, ancient building secrets of Middle Age church masons, etc. ... Upon my instigation, SS-Oberscharführer Otto Rahn participated in one of these discussions, being highly interested in the various mentioned areas. He also speaks fluent French. As far as SS-Oberscharführer Rahn was able to make his own observations about Mr. de Mengel's reported research on one of his earlier travels, he can confirm their accuracy." For translation of the work, Wiligut subsequently recommends Rahn and von Grönhagen, and for the evaluation of the mathematical part of de Mengel's work a mathematician,

---

1   Guénon, 244-248

preferably with "astrological and astronomical knowledge": SS-Sturmbannführer Frenzolf Schmid and for the evaluation of the "music-scientific works": Dr. Bose.[1] He refers here to the Berliner, Dr. Fritz Bose, who, in the Ancestral Heredity organization (SS-Ahnenerbe), was assigned the department for Nordic music, occupying himself with the faithful copying of Germanic musical instruments, the Lures.[2] Frenzolf Schmid was the author of a book about Atlantis published in 1931: "Original Texts of the First Divine Revelation – Attalantic Ur-Bible."

In a letter dated March 9, 1937, the staff of the SS-Reichsführer reacted to de Mengel's presence in Berlin: "The SS-Reichsführer acknowledges your letter of Febr. 19, 37. He wishes to first have Mr. de Mengel's works photocopied and then translated. The SS-Reichsführer agrees to various discussions with Mr. de Mengel in your house. He may wish to personally visit briefly with Mr. de Mengel again."[3]

On March 21, 1937, Schmid's opinion of de Mengel's mathematical works turned up. Schmid used the opportunity to call for, "the establishment of an academic teaching chair for Arian Wisdom."[4] Among other things, his opinion mentions: "The magnetic calculations of Mr. Professor DE MENGEL are built on ancient insights and are correct, but will unfortunately be hardly understood by today's still not accepted metaphysic's circle of the sciences ... It is safe to say that DE MENGELS observations, referencing the earlier literature, as well as the profundity of thought of the ATLANTEANS, the Germanic and Indo-Germanic peoples, thus reach consciously or unconsciously back to the Arian-Atlantisers WORLD CIRCLE, not only assumed by Germanic, but also by other Arian peoples."[5]

On April 26, 1937 Himmler receives from the division secretary "Idg.-finn Kulturbez." an overview of Gaston de Mengel's works including a short listing of contents.[6] In summary, de Mengel's text, "Europe's traditional Spirit, its Past and its Future" says: "[The author] highlights the superiority of the Middle Ages and the degenerative effect of the Renaissance. It observes the phases of traditional civilization in Europe: the bards, minstrels, troubadours, knightly orders, Templar orders, and their successors, the Rosenkreuzer, and provides the

---

1    Bundesarchiv (Germ. Fed. Arch.) NS 19, 3974, page 2 f.
2    Kater, 409, footnote 16
3    Germ. Fed. Arch. NS 19, 3974, page 5
4    Germ. Fed. Arch.19, 3974, page 8
5    Germ. Fed. Arch.19, 3974, page 9
6    Germ. Fed. Arch.19, 3974, page 18

true reason for the condemnation of the Tempel-Lords ringing the death knell of Western civilization ..."[1]

On May 4, 1937, Wolff is informed that de Mengel is "without any cash resources" and is asking for some monetary infusion in order to be able to pay for his return travel from Berlin to Paris, or to Helsingfors [Helsinki] to Mr. von Grönhagen, and for the past-due rent for his home in Paris. The SS-man responsible for the caretaking reported to Wolff: "I told him [de Mengel] that the SS-Reichsführer had scanned his works with interest, as far as he had been able to look at them, and would be pleased to once more speak with Mr. de Mengel ..."[2]

The German-Finn, Yrjö von Grönhagen, who had invited de Mengel to Berlin, was since February 1937 the head of the "Maintenance Organization for Indogerman-Finnish Cultural Relations" in the SS-Ancestral Heritage.[3] On May 22, 1937, Gaston de Mengel departed via Stettin from his visit with the SS to the Finnish capital, Helsinki.[4] With this, he decided to follow von Grönhagen,[5] who, by direction of the Ancestral Heritage was on a research trip to Finland.[6] It seems to indicate that de Mengel attached himself to von Grönhagen's assignment. Within the Ancestral Heritage, it was Grönhagen's task to search for "Parallels between Indo-Germans and Finns in order to establish a common origin."[7] Kater points out that, in this matter, "Himmler had assigned the Mongolian Finns a pure Germanic origin."[8] The intention was to establish the scientific inclusion of the Finns into the circle of Indo-Europeans imagining them as future allies in the final battle against the Semites. Considering that their language, shared only with Hungarian, that could not be traced back to Indo-Germanic – it was an, in principle, hopeless undertaking. However, since no publication of de Mengel's about Finland can be shown prior to his visit

---

1 Germ. Fed. Arch.19, 3974, pages 18-28
2 Germ. Fed. Arch.19, 3974, page 29 f.
3 Kater, 45, 78, 134, 193, 202, 286, 389. Grönhagen's Maintenance Department fell victim to the SS attempts to professionalize the Ahnenerbe. Von Grönhagen had no university degree, requiring him to leave. Right after the beginning of the war in 1939, Grönhagen cleared out to his Finnish home country.
4 Germ. Fed. Arch. NS 19, 3974, page 40
5 Lachner to Wolff, 4.5.37, BArch NS19-3974, P. 30
6 Kater, 78
7 Grönhagen, von: Approx. plan for the work of the Maintenance department for Indo-German-Finnish cultural relations, Berlin, Febr. 25, 1937, T-580, 206/717, citing Kater, 45 f.
8 Kater, 46

to Berlin (and subsequently), it would appear that his interest in his Helsinki stay was stirred up only in Berlin. Since his ship's passage to Helsinki was paid, an indirect assignment can be assumed.[1] According to the expense record, de Mengel presented to the SS the passport fees, two months rent for his Paris residence covering the time of his stay in Berlin, the rent in Berlin, and the Paris rent for a month in advance for the time of his return to Paris.[2] What caused de Mengel to travel to Berlin? Information is provided through a letter from the secretary of the SS-Ancestral-Heritage-Department "Maintenance Organization for Indo-German-Finnish Cultural Relations". On May 25, 1937, Ms. Gertraut Schlarb (de Mengel's translator in Berlin) wrote to the SS-Obersturmführer von Lachner at the Race and Settlement Main Office: "Honored Mr. von Lachner! As requested I am forwarding you a report on the various secret organizations. Mr. de Mengel was able to provide me only with this data, but will contact his friend, who knows much more, to supply further reports which I will then translate and immediately pass on to you."[3] De Mengel's work was financed by Himmler. With his travel itinerary he followed the interests of the Ancestral Heritage and reported about "Secret Organizations" – since he resided in Paris, these must have meant French secret organizations. However, a report on similar British organizations cannot be excluded, since, as is known, with de Mengel being British, he had published already in 1913 in the journal of the London Alchemist Society. All this indicates a classic intelligence service activity: At this time, de Mengel was acting as a spy for Germany – even if this is not stated anywhere. On which "Secret Organizations" might de Mengel have provided concrete information?

Gaston de Mengel is mentioned in a publication of Gérard de Sède.[4] The author presented publications on an illustrious subject spectrum – a spectrum covering the Templars as well as the Katharer or Fatima, and the village of Rennes-le-Château, located 40 km next to Carcassone in southern France. More exactly: De Sède wrote about the legends, concerning this village and his village priest Saunière who apparently had suddenly come into great wealth. The wealth, it was gossiped, could only have come about by the discovery of something very precious like ancient writings, gold or the Grail. Meanwhile,

---

1    Germ. Fed. Arch, NS 19-3974, page 39, Lachner to Winzer, use documentation for 600.00 reichsmark for de Mengel of May 24, 1937
2    Germ. Fed. Arch. NS 19-3974, page 32, Typescript *"Argent necessaire pour départ de M. Gaston de Mengel"*
3    Germ. Fed. Arch. NS 19-3974, page 43, Schlarb letter to Lachner of May 25, 1937
4    Acc. to Bnf.fr (French National Library) born 1921.

dozens of books exist on the subject, to which de Sède had already contributed in the '60s. In 1988, he followed up for a second time. In this book Gaston de Mengel is mentioned only in a single sentence: "*En 1924, en compagnie d'un certain Gaston Demengel, Georges Monti fonde le groupe occidental d'études ésotérique, dont le siège se trouve à Paris, 16, avenue de Viliers.*" ("In 1924, Georges Monti founded, together with a certain Gaston Demengel the 'Occidental Group for esoteric Studies,' with its seat located in Paris, Avenue de Villiers 16.")[1] He claims to have taken this from the foundation report of the group, prepared by George Monti. My request for inspection of this report remained, unfortunately, unanswered prior to this book's printing. However, since information about de Mengel is extremely rare, I will repeat with reservation de Sède's comments as follows. Following this report, this group had also a women's division, the Isis-Lodge, whose members could attain the ranks of "Dame" or "Fairy." The text supposedly contained a kind of manifesto, which pleaded for a reconciliation of the Churches and Initiation Centers, but poked fun at the wheelings-dealings of the American Rosenkreuzer, and in which there was a laudation on the students of the Egyptian Rite, "few scholars in the brotherhood ... [which is] known on the entire globe, not reaching a total number of 80 individuals, today, all of them occupied with mighty works for religious renewal and the laying of the foundation for a permanent peace across all western countries." Monti: "Our action will always be of a discreet nature, our lodges strictly closed to the uninitiated, our teachings closed especially to the curious and the prattlers, our ceremonies veiled to all ... A synthesis of undecided progress can establish itself only in the spirit of hierarchy and consequently may only be spread among elitist entities, truly superior spirits, chosen to civilize the people and to check the decadent currents."[2] These lines are supposedly signed by Marcus Vella, aka Monti. In this manifesto for the foundation of a group he had – according to de Sède – founded together with de Mengel, Monti admired a small group of insiders who occupied themselves with laying the "foundation for a permanent peace across all western countries." In the letter exchanged between Lachner and Himmler's personal staff with respect to de Mengel, it states, as a surprise to me and hardly understandable: "As I am learning from Ms. Schlarb [the translator], the SS-Reichsführer would greatly delight Mr. de Mengel if he would direct to him some lines of appreciation, in which he expresses that the SS-Reichsführer thanks him for providing his works and that he hopes that he will take from

---

1    Sède, 230
2    Sède, 230

Alexandre Saint Yves d'Alveydre:
"Zwölf Weise in Agarttha"
("Twelve Wise in Agarttha")
(Alveydre, 1886)

Josephin Péladan:
Rosenkreuzer
(Webb, Underground, 198)

Germany the impression that one is seriously intent on working on the promotion of European culture and European peace. Of course, this is entirely at the discretion of the Reichsführer."[1] De Mengel's request to receive such a letter of recommendation from a high-ranking German with respect to his works, may be understandable in the sense of collecting references, but why would he want to receive precisely in writing platitudes from the SS-Reichsführer about promotion of culture and peace? By themselves, such clichés would be in principle pointless to him. However, if it is implied that he acted on behalf of a group of people to whom these goals were explicitly important, such a letter (which de Mengel, by the way, never received[2]) would make sense, since it would make clear that

---

[1] Germ. Fed. Arch. NS 19-3974, page 30, Lachner letter to Wolff of May 4, 1937
[2] Lachner informed Wolff on May 24, 1937, following de Mengel's visit: "I have further told him [De Mengel] that the SS-Reichsführer would have transmitted his thanks in writing, but had, in consideration of Mr. de Mengel refrained from doing so, since such a letter could possibly have found abroad by a local administration in Mr. de Mengel' possession and could possibly have caused problems for Mr. de Mengel. Mr. de Mengel

de Mengel collaborated with a person that was not in opposition to the group's goals. The agreement of the goal of the supposed group of about 80 wise men of the Egyptian Rite, the securing of peace, with de Mengel's cliché, could be proof of de Mengel's membership in just this circle. But it must remain speculative.

Who was this Monti with whom de Mengel – according to de Sède – founded an esoteric circle, and what did he do? He is said to have been secretary of the famous occultist Joséphin Péladan. De Sède claims to have found more detailed information about Monti in a dossier of the clergyman Émile Hoffet. (having acquired parts of the Hoffet archives in 1966.) On orders of the Vatican,[1] Hoffet is supposed to have become active in spying on Monti. In this dossier it says: "Identity: Georges Monti, called Count ('Comte') Georges Monti, then Count Israêl Monti. Initiation name: Marcus Vella. German secret agent before World War I. National-Socialist secret agent after the war. He attained the highest rank of the Scottish Rite to supervise the activities. Converted to Judaism and 'Adopted Jew,' he became a member of the order B'nai B'rith (Jewish order similar to the Freemasons, founded in 1843 in the USA by ethnic German Jews under Henry Jones, as de Séde explains), achieved the grade 'Cohen' to spy there. Murdered in Paris on October 21, 1936 by poison and buried in silence ... Biography: Born in Toulouse in 1880, *Rue des Récollets,* adopted son of an Italian couple, who gave him away. Raised by Jesuits, chosen for the congregation, accepted to the theological college of the *Compagnie Jesu* in Avignon. He made foreign acquaintances in Toulouse. At age 24, he frequented the occult milieu with – possibly – acceptance into the secret society of the Katharer and Templar. ... Georges Monti displayed a vivid intelligence: Doctor of Canonical Church Rights of the Catholic Faculty of Paris. In alliance with Papus [Dr. Gérard Encausse (1865-1916)[2]], the revivor of Martinism, in alliance with the

---

realized this ... Mr. de Mengel has sent special thanks for the SS-Reichsführer's gift and the books." [Germ. Fed. Arch. NS 19-3974, page 40]

1    In 1864 Pope Pius IX, condemned in paragraph IV of the Syllabus errorum not only Socialism, but also the Societas clandestinae, the secret societies: *"Eiusmodi pestes saepe gravissimisque verborum formulis reprobantur in epistolis encycl. ..."* – "Such plagues are often and in grave expressions dismissed in encyclidies." (followed by a listing of old letters) [Mirbt, 451]

2    James Webb on Papus: "Papus was the pen name of Dr. Gérard Encausse (1865-1916), a member and often the instigator of many of the occult groups of his time. He had quarreled with the French Theosophists, with whom he had made an inauspicious debut; he was on the Supreme Council of Stantislas de Guita's Ordre Kabbalistique de la Rose-Croix; and he directed the leading French occult review, L'Initiation. His own particular specialties were Martinism ... and the propagation of the complicated theories

then celebrated Péladan, founder of the cabalistic Rosenkreuzer, and in alliance with Éduard Schuré [*1841 in Strasbourg, +1929], one of the directional men of Theosophy. Connections with Léon Daudet. (son of Alphonse Daudet, together with Charles Maurras, leader of the monarchist movement, *l'Action française*). In 1908 joined the Martinists, in whose hierarchy he quickly advances. In 1908 is in Egypt on behalf of Papus … 1909 accepted into the Bavarian Rosenkreuzer. Looking to make a living, he is employed in Paris as editor by the Freemason and general governor of Algeria, Luraud. In 1912 departure from Paris to Algiers … Frequently left Paris: Berlin, Rome. In Berlin participated in movies, won plenty of money."[1] So far de Séde/Hoffet about Monti.

A further source containing information about Monti can be found in the French occult scene, which, vs. de Séde has the advantage of being firsthand, and, in addition, is a contemporary source. The occultist Anne Osmont from Toulouse, follower of the Franciscans [1872-1952] wrote her memoirs in 1941. Under the title "My Remembrances – 50 Years of Occultism – My astral Travels," she also speaks of Monti in chapter entitled "My Relationship with the Freemasons": "My last adventure was clearly more serious. It was 1922. One day, I received a letter on bright yellow paper, like Péladan commonly used. It began with the words: 'My dear Sister in Jesus Christ'. and ended with to me an unknown signature: Vella Marcus. While reading, I recognized that Vella Marcus was the pseudonym of Georges Monti, the earlier secretary of Péladan, who wished to see me … He said that he requested my support for the renewal of the Templar Order. He said that he had been contracted by three German high lodges and enjoyed great support in Great Britain … While he spoke, I gained a totally different impression of Freemasonry. Until then, I had known only second class Freemasons, if I may say so, and had found them rather ridiculous. They met in temples whose symbols they did not understand … I now understood that Freemasons dealt with a comprehensive plan of destruction and rebuilding, which no less boiled down to destroying all that was dear and precious to me, only to establish, following the apocalypse and catastrophes, a society full of crazy ideas. To explain the value of the noble order, I would need to join, that which he called O.T.O. He mentioned the high-standing dignitaries who guided the order in the past and those that guided it now. The

---

of his ‚intellectual master', the Marquis de Saint-Yves d'Alveydre. Papus, in fact, held in his hands as many of the threads of French esotericism as he could possible manage. "
[Webb, Establishment, 168; see also André]

1   Sède, 226 ff.

officiating grand master was Alaister [sic] Crowley, whose knowledge he praised. Crowley truly possessed enormous knowledge, but the least I can say about him is, that Gilles de Rais [French serial killer, pederast, alchemist, +1440] was a rose, compared to Crowley; Crowley was a convinced and practicing satanist, or to say it more pointedly,'The Devil personified'." She cites Michel Demonforts article from the *"Réveil du Peuple"* of January 3, 1941: "In approximately 1937, Count Israel (Georges) Monti died suddenly in Rue du Rocher in Paris, after he had drunk a cup of tea. No Christian, yet Catholic, but several years earlier – according to confirmed statement – had converted to Judaism, to which he was totally attached ... Israel was a high initiate of occult world centers (Jewish, Freemason Centers, Asiatics, etc.), a member of the highest council of the Rosenkreuzer, at least one of his initiation names was Marcus Vella."[1] So far, Anne Osmont. Since de Mengel is only mentioned once by de Sède, and since his reference does not help to color Monti's picture any further, but with the information on Monti obviously corresponding with the true events and group constellations of the '20s, de Sède's statements are believable. It remains to say: in 1922 Monti attempted to have the known occultist, Anne Osmont, join the Ordo Templi Orientalis,[2] which, at that time was under the leadership of the notorious, Aleister Crowley. Two years later in Paris – according to de

---

1     Osmont, 61 ff.
2     James Webb on Ordo Templi Orientalis: "The most significant occult organization to be associated with Monte Verita was the magical society known as the Orden des Tempels des Ostens, otherwise, the Order of the Templars of the Orient. This society originated in a charter given by an English masonic entrepreneur called John Yarker to three German occultists: Joshua Klein, Franz Hartmann, and Theodor Reuss. This charter licensed them to set up in Berlin a Grand Lodge of the masonic rite called ‚Mizraim and Memphis' which Yarker had concocted from two moribund organizations. (By 1904 a fourth name and a new title were being mentioned in the magazine of the Order: Karl Kellner and the O.T.O.)" [Webb, Establishment, 59 f.] Theodor Reuss (1855-1924) shuttled frequently between Germany and England. In 1876 he joined the Freemasons in England. In 1886 he was expelled from the socialist league, since he supposed spied on it. In 1895 he became office manager at United Press in Berlin. [André, 146] Reuss wanted to prove that the major religions were established on the secret foundation of sexual magic and phallus cults. Reuss is said to have instructed a certain Dotzler about 1906 in a form of homosexual magic in a Munich hotel room. [André, 259] Lucien Sabah considers: *"Une autre question qui se pose, plutôt relative à antisémitisme qu'à l'antimaçonnisme, est de savoir si des homosexuels, nous en trouverons, ont été antisémites parce que cette pratique sexuelle est interdite dans le Pentateuqué (Lév. XVIII, 22.)"* [Sabah, 28] States: "Book Leviticus, IV. The Sacred Law, 18,22: "You must not have sexual relationship with a man as you do with a woman; it would be an atrocity."

Early seat of the I.P.A.-Institute, 13, Rue Béranger, Paris, where the British occultict Gaston de Mengel worked. In 1913, he composed an article about transformation of common metals into gold. In 1932 he wrote for the periodical of the "Polaires." He met Himmler in 1937. (Photos: 2004 Wegener)

Sède – the same Monti founded, with de Mengel, an occidental esoteric group. Edward Crowley (1875-1947) was in 1929 expelled from France for espionage.[1] Monti died in 1936, and a year later Monti's partner Gaston de Mengel met Heinrich Himmler in Berlin.

What other connections did de Mengel cultivate?

In 1929, de Mengel published a paper on the "Esoterics of Music" with the Paris publisher *"Bibliothèque Chacornac, 11, Quai Saint-Michel, 11."* This company had published numerous esoteric works. As is known, authors could be contacted through the publisher or the editorial department. Whether this happened or what other authors of the publisher became known to de Mengel in this way is unfortunately not known.

The same applies to magazines in which de Mengel was published. Thus, his article on the "Symbolism of the Trinity" published in *"Voile d'Isis"* in 1930 precedes, for instance, that of the later Nazi-collaborator Jean Marquès-Rivière.[2]

In 1925, a publication of de Mengel's is found in the newspaper *"Penser & Agir,"* issued by the I.P.A, the *"Institute de Psycho-Physique Appliquée,"* the institute for applied Psycho-Physics. In 1925, the institute was located at *"25, Rue des Apennins, Paris (17ᵉ),"* then, in 1926 at *"13, Rue Béranger, Paris (3ᵉ)."* The periodical was the voice of the *"Club Amical Penser & Agir."* In 1925, three gentlemen are named in *Penser & Agir* as being protagonists of the association: As the founder and general director: Louis Gastin. As director of the Paris service: Dr. Marcel Viard, and as the head of the Eutrophy-Service: Gaston de Mengel. In the same year, the change of the I.P.A. into a *"Société Anonyme par Actions,"* is announced with a starting capital of 50,000 francs. The *"Crédit Foncier d'Algérie et de Tunisie"* is chosen as the bank of issue. Who were de Mengel's colleagues in the administration of the I.P.A?

In 1921, Louis Gastin was the director of the journal "Sphinx" and the *"Université Synthétique Internationale – Université du Sphinx,"* which he had established in 1920 in Nice. "Sphinx" was, according to Gastin, a journal of *"Spiritualism integral,"* meaning a synthesis of philosophy, science and social issues. The journal was issued by the publisher *"Editions du Sphinx" 109, Quai des Etats-Unis,"* in Nice, whose address was identical with the University's. Besides Gastin as the director, Fernand Batel functioned as the journal's editor-in-chief,

---

1    Sabah, 26 f.
2    Page 156. Jean Marquès-Rivière, being Jean Marie Rivière [Trimondi, 277], 1903-2000 (bnf.fr)

who, simultaneously functioned as the *"Directeur-Adjoint des Services Administratifs"* of the University, with Jean Barral as its editorial secretary, responsible for economics and philology. Named as the main collaborators were: Pierre Borel, Dr. Breton, Léon Combes, L. Ferrand, R.-A. Fleury, Gabriel Gobron, Prof. J. Grialou, Daniel Isnard, F. Jollivet-Castelot, Albert Jounet (Alber Jhouney[1]), Paul Le Cour, Louis Le Leu, G. Melusson, Dr. G. Perisson, Raymond Perraud, G. Phaneg, Pierre Piobb, A. Porte-du-Trait-des-Ages, Alphonse Saltzmann, Oswald Wirth,[2] and others.

Gastin wrote the foreword to the book *"La Pensée – son méchanisme et son action"* which appeared in 1921. It was written by today's best known French esoteric in the 19th century, who, by that time had already died, Dr. Gérard Encausse, called Papus. It appeared in Gastin's Sphinx publishing house. Gastin's foreword becomes a posthumous laudatio to Papus's life and work, stating that he had created a remarkable synthesis of antique insights and modern, scientific concepts. The revivor of occultism had known how to transmit by analogy scientific, philosophical, and metaphysical truths to all mankind. So far Gastin about Papus. Attached to the publication – probably for advertising among Papus fans – was the founding manifesto of the Sphinx University: The separatism of the diverse spiritual schools caused a condition of inferiority in the face of unified materialism, requiring a totally independent synthesis from the specialized individual teachings, precisely the *Université Synthétique Internationale*. It was to be a cooperative of the mind to which all intellectuals were invited, all idealists, who were being squashed morally and materially by an enormous wave of egotism. According to the *"Règlement Général"* of the University, it was established by private initiative. There were three kinds of members: The honorary members by force of their moral contribution and those who were kindly providing financial support. The producers, who maintained the various

---

1 Acc. to bnf.fr (1860-1926)
2 James Webb on Oswald Wirth: "Huysmans had discovered the Abbé Boullan while researching material on Satanism for his novel Là-bas. In the summer of 1891 the novelist had gone to stay with Boullan in Lyon. He attended ceremonies in the Abbé's sanctuary, at which his host had used the rites of Vintras to combat the machinations of his enemies in Paris, Bruges, and Rome. Among these enemies were Stanislas de Guaita, his future secretary, Oswald Wirth, and a fellow occultist, Joséphin Péladan ... In 1879 Oswald Wirth had met Boullan at Châlons-sur-Marne, where Wirth enjoyed some reputation as a magnetizer. Boullan had appeared in the town and performed a miraculous cure. Wirth and he then entered into correspondence. With the connivance of the Abbé Roca, another priest defrocked for heresy, Wirth began to worm from Boullan his most secret doctrines." [Webb, Underground, 156 f.]

departments, and the ordinary members, who, without discrimination against their sex, faith, race or nationality were allowed to pay annual dues. Planned or even realized were laboratories for hermetic studies, a library and a reading room, experimental séances and conversations, the bulletin of the university, a medical and astrological service, and, among others, departments for sociology, hypnosis, tradition, esoteric, mysticism, metaphysics and initiation. In addition, there would be local, regional and international subsidiaries of the University. The organization's plan names: Local groups in Paris and Bordeaux, and an attached *"Société de Culture Morale et de Recherches Psychiques"* in Carcassonne; in addition, there were regional arrangements in Angouleme, Avignon and Marseilles; overseas in Egypt was Charles Brun, teacher at the French Institute of Fine Arts in Alexandria, and in Spain Juan de Nogalès in Madrid and Albert Vechi in Alicante.

Gastin's founding of the university in 1920 may have been a response to his resignation from the Theosophical Society in March of 1919. He had been a member since December of 1915 and *"Premier Secrétaire de la Branche 'Agni'."* At the time, his contact partner with the theosophics of Marseilles/Nice was *"Madame la Comtesse Prozor,"* who resided at the *"Maison-Rose"* in Nice with whom he, however, was less at loggerheads than with Monsieur Charles Blech, the general secretary of the Theosophical Society of France.[1]

During his membership with the theosophes he had already founded the *"Institute des Hautes Sciences"*, together with Albert Jounet.[2] He had gotten to know Jounet ten years earlier in the Parisian spiritist milieu at an occultist congress. The *"Institute des Hautes Sciences"*, regardless of certain doctrines or schools, was intended to openly dedicate itself liberally and openly to all searchers of free

---

1   Gastin, 9 f.
2   James Webb on Albert Jounet: "The influence of Péladan was most marked in the field of the visual arts. After the War of the Two Roses [Stanislas de Guaita with the Ordre Kabbalistique de la Rose-Croix / Péladan (aka "Sâr Mérodak") with the Ordre de la Rose+Croix Catholique du Temple et du Graal], the Sar established his triple Order of the Rose-Croix-Catholique, the Temple, and the Grail. His chief colleagues in this venture were Albert Jounet, Elémir Bourges ... Jounet had originally been a member of de Guaita's order; he was a Cabalist and a symbolist poet ... From writing books on the Zohar he became more and more Catholic, founded the Fraternité de l'étoile, a lay mystical order, and gradually drew away from Péladan. His friend, Elémir Bourges, had undergone a phase of lavish dandyism ... but he had taken refuge from this too strenuous existence in a black pessimism and a chair in the Bibliothèque Nationale where he ,read everything'." [Webb, Underground, 179 f.]

methods of the occult.[1] Attached to it was the magazine *"L'Etoile,"* founded at the same time in 1889 with the *"Fraternité de l'Etoile,"* the "Brotherhood of the Star" (both by Albert Jounet). In 1919, the journal was under the leadership of Louis Gastin. In his polemical writing of 1919 *"Comment on Entre dans la Société Théosophique – Comment on en Sort"* ("How one joins the Theosophical Society – and how one resigns from it"), Gastin settles accounts with the Theosophes. In 1899, it was said that he turned to spiritualism and in 1903, to the occult sciences. In light of his many years of experience, it was clear to him that one would always remain a student in the area of occult studies, this field of studies being infinitely large. He therefore fought against all narrowing into partial studies and special instructions. This is why there could never be masters in Theosophy or in occultism, only guides or students who could be a small step ahead. But Blavatsky's theosophy was no universal theosophy, but a neo-buddhist, Oriental theosophy, rather he pursued an *occidental*, that is Western theosophy.[2] Most adherents of the Oriental-oriented theosophy of Blavatsky's were said to be Christians, who, under the influence of natural-philosophy, pantheistic-Buddhist teaching had become anti-Christian. Gastin sees himself as the defendant of the occidental-Judeo-Christian tradition. He warns of an assimilation of Christianity by Buddhism, which he sees advancing in the West behind the mask of a false Christianity in light of the theosophical spread of Buddha's apostulate. The promotion of Christian esotericism is said to have been the goal of the *"Fraternité de l'Etoile,"* founded in 1889 by Jounet. This was said to have been also the goal of its Christian movement, which did not intend to force Christianity onto the world, but would, at the same time, not see it simply annexed: "Theosophs, you can gladly be Buddhists … but do not deform Christianity."[3] Had he known of the absolute identification of the society with Blavatsky's teachings, he would have never joined, especially since the society pursued a dogma, even if it was not called that … In this brochure, he was focusing on the reasons for his resignation, so as not to become the objects of slander – as it had happened already to other departed occultists before him. The brochure therefore pursued an exclusively prophylactic goal, designed only to protect himself.[4]

---

1  Gastin, 6
2  Gastin, 3 f.
3  Gastin, 6 f.
4  Gastin, 1 f.

Gastin spoke much more positively about the Martinists:[1] "The Martinist Order accepted into its innermost circle even morally good materialists and asked of its members only one thing, the recognition of the universal principle of brotherhood: The sincere and selfless pursuit of truth."[2] This praise for the Martinists suggests a simultaneous or subsequent membership. Webb writes about the Martinists: "In France, Papus revived the Martinist Order, or more precisely: He invented it."[3] Incidentally, the Martinists are also mentioned by William Butler Yeats in his autobiography. In 1896, he describes the following experience in Paris: "I am smoking haschisch with several adherents of Saint-Martin, the mystic of the eighteenth century. At one o'clock in the morning, while we were talking crazy stuff with several of us dancing, there was a knock on the closed window shutters. We opened them and three ladies enter, the wife of a writer, thinking to find an accomplice, and the two younger sisters of her husband she had secretly taken to a disreputable ball. She is very confused upon seeing us, but while looking from one to the other, she notices that we have taken narcotics, and laughs. Caught up by our dreams, we recognize indistinctly that she is by our and every other moral code a scandalous person, but we smile at her kindly and laugh."[4]

So far Louis Gastin. Who was the other leading member of the I.P.A. besides Gaston de Mengel? Doctor Marcel Viard (1884-1979) lived in 1928 at

---

[1] Differentiate between *l'Ordre Martiniste,* headed from 1934 to 1939 by Chevillon (Lyon), and the *Ordre Martiniste & Synarchique* under Victor Blanchard. [Sabah, 258]

[2] Gastin, 17 f.

[3] Webb, Underground, 275

[4] Yeats, 333. James Webb on the belief about occult arbiter in the background of world affairs and the Martinists: "Eventually arose the legend – which always lives behind occult Masonry – that there were ‚Secret Chiefs' – ‚Unknowns Superiors' – who held themselves aloof from the normal affairs of the Brotherhood, but were themselves in possession of the ultimate secrets. (This was to become a common occult doctrine. The Theosophical Masters derived from the same theory.) Partly responsible for this train of thought were the Martinist Orders of speculative Masonry, which stemmed from the teachings of Martinès de Pasqually (died 1774), the founder of the Order of the Elus Coëns. This Order died with its founder's death. But the idea of Hidden Chiefs survived in the doctrines of other speculative Orders, carried by the chief disciple of Martinès de Pasqually, J.-B. Willermoz, a leading mover in Masonic politicking of the 18th century, and a believer in Hidden Chiefs who were actually supernatural. There were other occult orders and many other supporters of the ‚Hidden Chiefs', particulary in Germany and Sweden; but Martinist doctrines, transmitted either by Willermoz through Masonry, or through the teachings of his fellow-disciple, Louis-Claude de Saint Martin, stand as the type for others." [Webb, Underground, 226]

ZAM BHOTIVA

# ASIA MYSTERIOSA

*L'Oracle de Force Astrale
comme moyen de communication avec
« Les Petites Lumières d'Orient »*

PRÉCÉDÉ D'UNE PRÉFACE DE F. DIVOIRE
ET D'ÉTUDES PAR MAURICE MAGRE ET J. MARQUÈS-RIVIÈRE

**DORBON-AINÉ**
19, Boulevard Haussmann, 19
**PARIS**

United: SS-Collaborator Jean Marquès-Rivière and the man who induced Otto Rahn to the Search for the Grail, Maurice Magre, as well as the member of the "Polaires," Zam Bhotiva (1929)

11, *Rue du Printemps, Paris (17e)*.[1] A writer, he researched the causes of war. In *"Le Naturisme et la Guerre"* (1928), he argued that minerals attack minerals, plants destroy plants, animals kill animals, why then not also people against people? Maybe, it was a quite normal occurrence, something natural, one had to respect. War could be compared with an illness. The soldiers (the lymphocytes of society) would light the fire to maintain the endangered state. But naturism could fight the true causes of war, the gaping wounds.[2] Dr. Viard was a medical doctor, a specialist of psychotherapy and a Freemason. Member (1950) of the *"Grand Collège des Rites," "Grand Commandeur"* (1955-1958), and finally *"Grand Commandeur d'honneur as vitam."*[3]

In addition to the contacts with his I.P.A.-colleagues, de Mengel maintained also contacts with the esoteric group of the *'Polaires'*, since he published a serial article[4] about the allegory of the Trinity in the *"Bulletin des Polaires"* in May, June, July, and August of 1932.[5] The setting up of the periodical, the bulletin, and its use was ordered for the group of Wise Men from Tibet by means of a new oracle method. The oracle's goal for the group says that the bulletin was to be the report on the studies and works of the Polars."[6] Publications in the bulletin by nonmembers was therefore excluded in principle by dictate of higher powers. This not only urgently suggests a firm collaboration of de Mengel with the *"Polaires"* beyond the article series, but even his membership in the group. Otto Rahn, too, maintained connections with at least one of the Polars: Maurice Magre. Accordingly, it cannot be excluded that the SS heard through Rahn of de Mengel. Rahn was also roped into looking after de Mengel during his stay in Berlin. But this remains speculative. Who were the "Polaires" in whose membership periodical de Mengel published?

The "Polars" were an occidental esoteric group, who claimed to have been in contact with a spiritual center in Tibet via a new oracle method. The oracle

---

1 Viard, Marcel: *Le Naturisme et la Guerre,* Paris 1928 [Protocol of a conference on May 26, 1928 at *Salle Jouffroy*, Paris]
2 Viard, ibid.
3 Ligou, Daniel, Article : Viard, Marcel, in: *Dictionaire de la franc-maçonnerie, Nouvelle Edition 1987*, Paris [Presses Universitaires de France, First edition 1974]
4 Unfortunately, this article cannot be bibliographically captured, but, considering the subject, ought to closely resemble de Mengel's exposition of the trinity in the French esoteric magazine *"Voile d'Isis,"* The "Veil of Isis," in 1929-30.
5 Germ. Fed. Arch.NS 19-3974, page 22, Compilation of de Mengel's publications
6 Bhotiva, 146

functioned by assigning letters to numbers, which were then modified by different, calculated steps. The result was again converted to letters. *Et voilà*: The answer to the question that was earlier converted from text to numbers, now stood out in black and white on the paper of the one who had asked the questions. But how did those responsible get the conversion key? Well, a hermit, Brother Julien, living near Rome, had been so kind as to explain the procedure to a later member of the group, only to disappear afterwards. Even the title of the text that appeared in December of 1929, in which the procedure was explained, had before been determined by the oracle: *"Asia Mysteriosa"* – "Mysterious Asia." The book was written by a diverse group of people, with the Italian Zam Bhotiva primarily responsible. Standing by him were Maurice Magre, who had given Otto Rahn the idea for the search of the Grail near Montségur, and Jean Marquès-Rivière who was destined to later assume an important role in the surveillance and persecution of French secret organizations in the area occupied by Germany. Fernand Divoire contributed a two-page foreword.

The core ideas of the text were by no means new at the time of the book's printing. In 1886, *"Mission de l'Inde en Europe – Mission de l'Europe en Asie"* by Saint-Yves d'Alveydre had already appeared. The book contained statements about the supposed existence of an occult dedication center, called Agartha, in Asia. The Marquis Saint-Yves d'Alveydre died on Febr. 5, 1909. Subsequently, Gérard Encausse (Papus) founded the *"Société des Amis de Saint Yves,"* with the goal of reeding his works and to publish whatever was still unpublicized in the possession of his heirs, the Comtesse Keller and Comte Alexander Keller. The new edition in 1910[1] with the original title had first appeared in 1886, but had been quickly withdrawn. In his book, the Marquis wrote about the sacred territory, Agartha, that he – as indicated by friends of the Marquis in the new edition – claimed to have gotten to know first by research, and then through his own astral journeys. James Webb explained astral journeys as follows: "The process of astral journeys, by which some occultists claim to depart from their physical bodies, and then travel about in their astral bodies."[2] The Marquis placed Agartha in the Himalayas, however, it was *"introuvable"* – untraceable. He claimed that the sacred territory had almost four million residents.[3] Many

---

1  Tappa, Gilbert; Boumendil, Claude, *"Notes des Editeurs"* (1981), in: Alveydre, 5. To the possible idea providers of the Marquis maybe like Fabre d'Olivet (who also inspired Blavatsky [Webb, Establishment, 499]): Saunier, Jean: *Introduction: Une Etrange Histoire*, in: Alveydre, I ff.
2  Alveydre, Avertissement of "Freunde," Pl. Vf.; Webb, Underground, 174
3  Alveydre, 54 f.

of the city's buildings were supposedly underground.¹ Twelve masters possessed the highest ordination.² Furthermore, there was a supreme Pontifex of Agartha.³ D'Alveydre also dedicated a longer passage to a description of the Ether: "The unspeakable substance, the sacred element that served the eternal and its divine faculties, as Char. This substance is called in all our languages Ether or Akasa in Sanskrit. I herewith point out to the reader everything that I have written in the *'Mission des Juifs,'* the 'Mission of Jews'. The Ether is a living element, beguiling in an unspeakable way and of a sacred intoxication, entirely spiritual, but still leaving the intelligence in sufficient control to maintain individual consciousness and to keep the body, although with difficulty, in an excited condition."⁴

In 1924, Saint-Yves d'Alveydre's work was broadly plagiarized by Ferdinand Ossendowski. The German title was: *"Tiere, Menschen und Götter"* – "Animals, People, and Gods." In 1929, Saint-Yves d'Alveydre's work, as well as Ossendowski's, was drawn on by the Polars for their own publication *"Asia Mysteriosa"* and broadly used as a model. The only new claim with was to have found a reliable means of communication, which had already been claimed by the literary predecessors, Asiatic-occult powers – and that without the need for a stressful journey to Asia. Since Gaston de Mengel published in the bulletin, founded according to the instructions of the star oracle, an examination of the Polars' expositions about the oracle, its emergence and its prophesies, makes perfect sense. All the more, since Himmler, when he met de Mengel in 1937, already knew the core idea of the Polar myths and about one of the two literary precursor's of the book: Ossendowski's "Animals, People, and Gods," which he had read in 1924. He commented on the book as follows: "The Story of an American and his Flight east from Siberia through Tibet and Mongolia. – Bolshevik atrocities and then the very great mysteries and secrets of Mongolia. – Further about Baron von Ungern-Sternberg."⁵ Himmler has therefore – since he, opposite to numerous examples from his reading list, abstained from any critique – had accepted the "Great Mysteries" Ossendowski spread, uncritically.

Here are some excerpts from "Animals, People, and Gods": "On my journey through Central Asia, I heard for the first time of the Mysterium of Mysteries ... Old people on the banks of the Amyl River told me that, following an old

---

1   Alveydre, 61
2   Alveydre, 62
3   Alveydre, 66
4   Alveydre, 124 f.
5   Himmler, Leseliste (Reading list), Title 213, page 31

legend, a certain Mongolian tribe, in order to escape Ghengis Khan's demands, had hidden in the subterranean land. A Sojot ... showed me the smoking gate, supposedly representing the entrance to the kingdom of Agharti ... 'Everything in the world', said the Gelong, 'finds itself in a continuous state of change ... More than sixty-thousand years ago, a saint, together with an entire tribe of people, disappeared into the earth, never to return again to the surface ... no one knows, where the kingdom is located. Some say in Afghanistan, others in India ... The sciences developed quietly there ... the land below the earth is now a great kingdom. Millions of people belong to it ...' Count Chultun Beyle added: 'This kingdom is Agharti ... You know that there existed two continents in the two greatest oceans of east and west that disappeared below the water surface. Their inhabitants belong now to the subterranean kingdom ...' The Torguten-Lama ... gave me further details: 'The residents of Agharti can drain oceans, turn continents into oceans, and turn mountains into desert dust ...'"[1] The Hutuktu of Narabantschi supposedly told Ossendowski of the following prophesy from the Kingdom of Agharti: "More and more people will forget their souls and think of their physical well-being ... A terrible battle will erupt among all people. The ocean will turn red ... The earth and the bottom of the seas will be covered by bones ... The enemies of God and the divine spirit in man will come ... Of ten thousand people only one will remain ..."[2] So what were the thoughts of the Polars who fell back on Ossendowski?

In *"Asia Mysteriosa"*, Zam Bhotiva says that the transmission of the oracle method took place in Bagnia in 1908, a hamlet in Viterbais, a Roman province [to the north of Rome], where a mysterious hermit whom the locals called Father Julien, had lived. Father Julien supposedly entrusted the Starpower-Oracle to "our friend" at a time when he was totally, worldly oriented, if not hostile towards all occult things.[3] In 1909, Father Julien, who surely wore the symbol of the rose and the cross under his coat of coarse wool, disappeared, supposedly having returned to a monastery in the Himalayas. Some of the messages that had been transmitted by the oracle were claimed to have been signed in his name; other messages had been signed by other entities.[4] The information by the oracle provided us with the certainty that the method constituted a milestone – real and tangible – by fate placed onto the secret path of the occult. But now the

---

1    Ossendowski, 344-348
2    Ossendowski, 358 f.
3    Bhotiva, 35
4    Bhotiva, 57

time had come, when this stone would serve as a guide, as a new *"Etoile Polaire,"* as a new Pole Star, those who felt lost in the darkness of Earth.[1] However, the secret of the method could not be revealed. A communication in July of 1929 told us that, when the group of Polars, at that time being constituted, would be reconstructed, and the oracle's method would be given by its present owner to a Polar who would be designated at a later point in time.[2]

Maurice Magre, Otto Rahn's acquaintance in Paris,[3] in his chapter of *"Asia Mysteriosa"*, elaborated on "a means of communication with the masters." According to his contemporaries, this way was commonly thought to be absurd, erroneous, and careless. They believed only if there was proof; everything new was laughed at. However, he thought that it was also necessary to be antiscientific, and to honestly make the method of credulity one's own. To read the respective book required one to temporarily suspend his belief. To him, the fact of a method of communication with people living in the Himalayas and the receipt of advice, philosophical aperçus concerning the world, and the partial prediction of the future by these wise beings, based on numbers, appeared by no means exceptional. He suggested that he had found his personal opinions confirmed in contact with the community of those, who were more highly enlightened than us, who had attained a higher degree of evolution, living in the solitude Tibet's. The existence of this brotherhood, called from time to time Agartha and the Great White Lodge, was known for a long time. The foundation of the theosophical movement by Madame Blavatsky in 1875 was, according to his opinion, absolute and certain proof for the existence of a spiritual center in the Himalayas.[4] And yes, even on Earth were they to have a, to us, unknown organization, wherein they were grouped according to their spiritual and moral rank. At the very top of their hierarchy stood the three Higher Wise Men. They guided the others, they being the Three Wise of Agarttha, of whom the book speaks by calling them the Great Lights. Maybe, the truth of the Orient, the wisdom guarded in the oldest buildings of Himalayan monasteries, had reached us.[5]

Magre was otherwise very active as an author. For instance, in 1935, he published *"La Clef des Choses Cachées"* – "The Key to the secret Things" through the publishing house, *"Bibliothèque-Charpentier"*,[6] a collection of statements on

---

1     Bhotiva, 31 f.
2     Bhotiva, 36
3     Lange, Rahn, 30 ff., 234
4     Bhotiva, 9-12
5     Bhotiva, 16
6     Fasquelle Éditeurs, 11, Rue de Grennelle

# MAURICE MAGRE

# LA CLEF
### DES
# CHOSES CACHÉES

La Sagesse des Druides — Le Svastika
L'Héritage des Albigeois — Merlin l'Enchanteur
La Légende du Graal — Le Mystère des Tarots
L'Arche d'alliance des Juifs — La Mission des Bohémiens
Le secret du Bouddha et celui de Jésus

PARIS
BIBLIOTHÈQUE-CHARPENTIER
FASQUELLE ÉDITEURS
11, RUE DE GRENELLE, 11

Maurice Magre, member of the Polaires, who distanced himself from racism in Germany.

almost all the classic subjects of esotericism. He wrote, for instance, about the swastika: "The swastika stands for the power of time. When it became a purely Buddhist symbol, it symbolized the wheel of life to which man is chained and from which he can free himself only by means of purification. In our days its meaning has totally changed. In Germany, it now stands for race hatred and the greed for violence."[1] "There are different interpretations for the swastika. Burnouf sees a fire symbol in it. Max Muller, that of the sun, G. d'Alviella, that of the moon, Madame Blavatsky, that of the initiation center of the world, René Guénon sees in it the symbol of the pole."[2] In fact, Guénon formulates in his classic "The King of the World": "We want to direct attention especially to the following: the center meant here, is the firm point which all traditions call in concurring symbolism the pole, since the world revolves around it in a circular movement, generally represented by the Celts as well as the Chaldeans and Hindus in the form of a wheel. This is the true meaning of the swastika, spread everywhere from the farthest East to the extreme West. By its nature, it is the 'symbol of the pole'. This, is its true meaning, which is doubtlessly shown for the first time in contemporary Europe."[3]

---

1   Magre, 28
2   Magre, 32
3   Guénon, König, 20. Guénon wrote about the "Pole," as whose symbol he gave here the swastika, also in other places. He cites for it a text about the Jewish Kabbala: Vulliaud, P.: "La Kabbale juive," I, 492,499: "'The expression Metatron includes all meanings of custodian, lord, envoy, mediator.' It is 'the originator of theophanies in the visible world,' the 'Angel of the countenance,' also the 'prince of the world' (Sar ha-olam) ... To use the handed down symbolism, as we explained before, we want to designate Metatron as the 'heavenly pole,' as the hierarchal head of the initiated is the 'earthly pole.' This pole finds its reflection by which he stands in immediate relationship on the 'world axis'." [Guénon, König, 28] Upon the establishment of earthly initiation centers general-topographic peculiarities and the "spiritual influences" ought to be observed. Guénon calls this new work area "'sacred geography'" [Guénon, König, 36] In chapter "Omphalos und Betyl" of his "König der Welt," Guénon places Agartha truly on the north pole: "As reported already, Agartha carried a different name at the beginning. It was called Paradesha ... Paradise ... Incidentally, according to certain texts of the Veda and Avesta, this area supposedly was literally located in the sense of the word at the pole." [Guénon, König, 64 f.] Julius Evola, who also made his acquaintance with the oracle of the Polars, judged about the location of the mystical world center: "The Gral is a nordic mystery, since the doctrine of the highest world center, as well as the most important elements of the Gral's symbolism refer back to the hyperboraic tradition. This tradition is much older ... than the ... Indo-Germanic, i.e. Arian tradition ..." [Evola, Gral, 8 f.] Evola, referring to Guénon, concerning the "Weihe der arischen Kasten" [Evola, Erhebung, 456] as well as directly from the "König der Welt." [Evola, Erhebung, 176] Evola: "Especially the reciprocal influence

Guénon, was to have worked originally with the Polaires.[1] Magre writes about the initiation center and its Wise Men: "The most wonderful hypothesis is that they [the Wise Men] certify a divine origin. Certain occultists claim that the Wise Men are far ahead of us in their development, residing on the planet Venus; they supposedly were dispatched to Earth to transmit to man the basics of knowledge. These delegates had instructed students who, in turn, conveyed knowledge to others. All the world knows Agarttha ... of which Ossendowski speaks. Saint d'Alveydre ... confirmed that Agarttha ... is truly extant and active, even if subterranean ... René Guénon says that Agarttha is the 'Earth of Immortality', but not always invisible. Supposedly, Agarttha is [presently] invisible only because we find ourselves in a period of darkness, the Kali Yuga.[2] But a time would come, when the Initiates would reappear ..."[3] A transmission touching on that of Agarttha, is to be the story of Atlantis, an island devoured by a great cosmic catastrophe. But there were people who escaped, and who had made it their task to preserve the moral inheritance of mankind. They supposedly found refuge on the peaks of the Himalayas. From there they returned to the, by then, barbaric-turned world. The magicians of the Chaldeans, the Orphikers of Greece, the Esseners of Palestine, the Pythagorans, the Egyptian Therapeuts,[4] the Gallic Druids, they were all claimed to have been societies of this order. The Druids had truly come from a center located in Ireland, that again had been

---

between the arctic subject and the atlantic subject must be emphasized, the secret of the north and the secret of the west, for the residence that followed the traditional ur-pole, was supposedly the atlantic. It is known from the astrophysical-dependent inclination of the Earth's axis that, from time to time, a climate shift results." [Evola, Erhebung, 177] "The Tibetan tradition transmits accordingly the memory of Tchang Sambhala, the mystical 'City of the North' ... " [Evola, Erhebung, 179] "... and that by a cosmic plan. We rather limit ourselves to the observation that, since the shift of the polar region this increasing self-distortion and shedding of tradition is noticeable which, following the 'cyclical laws' in the iron or dark epoch – kali-yuga – ... is to peak, to which lastly the modern times belong in the narrower sense." [Evola, Erhebung, 181]

1 Guénon, 447-448 (acc. to Godwin, 89)
2 The dark epoch of Kali Yuga is described in Vishnu Purana (India): "Slave races will become rulers of the world; leaders will be violent by nature; instead of protecting their subjects, they will rob them; the sole connection between the sexes will be lust; the Earth will be valued only for its raw materials; ... the one who disperses the most money will dominate mankind ..." [Waterfield, 88 – the author motivates his problems with democracy spiritually: Waterfield, 96] Opinions diverge about the beginning, end, and duration of this period.
3 Magre, 34 f.
4 The Egyptian therapists were Jewish hermits.

originally promoted from Asia, as the similarity between the organization of the Druids and the organization of the Lamas proved.[1] By 1220, there was to have still existed a secret shrine at the Irish Kildare, where an eternal fire burned maintained by virgins who were called the Daughters of Fire. Supposedly, concurrent with the extinguishing of this flame, there was the destruction of the Katharer by the crusade of Innocent the III in Midi of France.[2] There was to have been a spiritual transmission from the Druids to the Katharer. Numerous proofs confirmed the transfer of knowledge from the Himalayas: In the orphic poetry verses are found which, word for word, seem to be translated from the Veda-hyms. A biography of Buddha's had made its rounds in the West in the 11th and 12th century, the Christian version of which was said to be the novel of Barlaam and of Joasaph. Supposedly, the renunciation formula that had been demanded in Byzanz by the Katharers had been rediscovered, and Buddha's name had stood next to that of Manis. This may convince all those who want to support the idea that Buddhism's line of thought would not be found in Katharism. A wisdom, always the same, had circulated among mankind and had always conveyed the same message: the soul was immortal and in order to regain the divine condition, it had to pass through many lives.

Magre spoke also briefly in his chapter about the Grail of his old acquaintance, Otto Rahn, a "young German writer with talent." Critically, he noted that Rahn attested – without providing any proof – that there was no connection between Buddhism and Katharism. His book "Crusade against the Grail" was said to have nevertheless been written with love and provided rich documentation.[3] Magre repeated in his book the assumption he had earlier expressed verbally to Rahn, that the Grail had "as is said" been created in the grotto of Ornolac.[4] He later finds a less material explanation for the Grail: The confirmation of the Katharer, the Consolamentum, the comforting of the faithful, had been Jesus's secret and the spirit of the Grail.[5]

Were it possible to gather all the wise men, like the Tibetan monks, the Druids, or the Katharer of Montségur by circumventing the laws of time, they would effortlessly understand each other according to Magre. And, possibly, the members of this impossible- to-realize gathering would be dressed in the same

---

1    Magre, 35-37
2    Magre, 70
3    Magre, 110
4    Magre, 138
5    Magre, 148

way, in white linen cloth, representing purity. They would all order the same for their meals. And at the hour when the sun had not risen yet but was soon to rise, they would all perform the same rite. The white-clad people would, no matter at what place or time, stand upright with their faces turned east to greet the morning's light like the coming of the spirit. And by force of the appeal, the spirit would have descended into them. Magre posits the question, whether there are still people today who at sunrise would call on the rising spirit: "And if they exist, where are they?"[1] He later called the Rosenkreuzer the heirs of the Katharer.[2]

Jean Marquès-Rivière explains in his chapter on the oracle's method – the conversion of the letters of questions to numbers and their calculation with the subsequent reversal of the numerical results to letters and with that to legible answers, that this method showed no reference with the also numerically based cabalistic methods which, as answers, knew only "Yes" or "No." Among the [spiritualist] methods, there was none, he claims, that showed the richness, flexibility, and complexity of the Star Power Oracle. He did not doubt the reality of the oracle, since the obtained answers often contradicted the expectations of the questioner or operator [who processed the calculations] and since often incomprehensible answers were given [to the operator] in Sanskrit. The decisive criterion for the evaluation of the oracle was otherwise the output: The tree is judged by its fruit.[3] The received instructions that did not contradict Western spiritualism. Still, there's the question for the existence of large, traditional [Initiation-] Centers in Europe. To him, it seemed to have been resolved a long time ago. Since the 17th century, since the signing of the Westfalian Treaty in 1648, which had demonstrated remarkable religious importance, it seemed that there was no longer any sign of the presence of any initiation center in the West. Piece by piece, materialism had conquered the realm of metaphysics, followed by philosophy and things of a religious nature. According to a persevering transmission, the last representatives of the western initiation centers, who had often been caught under the name of the Rose-Cross, had fled to the Orient at the time. Marquès-Rivière names Swedenborg and Anna-Katherina Emmerick as chief witnesses of this idea, who had both referred to the wise men in Tibet. That communication with the oracle happened in the western way and was attributed to it [for after all, it dealt with former western wise men, according to

---

1     Magre, 74
2     Magre, 149
3     Bhotiva, 20

Marquès-Rivière, who had fled to Asia]. He then becomes principled: "Who are we? Nothing. Personal freedom ... may be important from a personal perspective. From a cosmic perspective, it is not. The commands seem to be given. Agents of mighty power appear to receive them as people and like the marionettes of a clown show, execute them ... There are the angels of light and the angels of darkness. At a given point in time, a decision must be made: 'The lukewarm will be spit out'. ["Because you are tepid, I shall spit you out" – Revelation of St. John 3, 16 (Apocalypse)] ... Oddly enough, all this is also confirmed by the final oracle messages in 1929, referring to the 'Reconstruction' of a group by the name of 'Polaire', whose esoteric rules are precisely 'ordered' with the help of this method. The Asian Center *wants* a center in Europe: and I do not doubt that 'They,' considering their colossal power, will get what they desire. The extraordinary phenomena occurring at this time, ascertain my position," so said Marquès-Rivière.[1]

Zam Bhotiva also highlights the foundation of a group, or rather the *Reconstruction* of a group by the name of 'Polars.'" The oracle's instructions are: *"Formez le Groupe des ‚Polaires' et faites-lui par-courir le Monde."*[2] ("Establish the group of Polars and let them overrun the world.") How this is to happen is not more closely defined in the detailed goals of the group: "– To overrun the world by means of a bulletin, a message statement becoming the report of the Polars' studies and works."[3] Further goals of the group were dictated as follows: "– By all means, fight the foolish fear of death that troubles reason. Why tremble, when they will go through a better gate? Why close their eyes when facing the Light? ... - Protection and help for children that grow up without love. This mission is entrusted to the leader of the women's group ... - Establishment – by patient work – of centers in all parts of the world, centers serving the formation and organization of Polars ... – All Polars will find help and advice from their leaders who, in cases of doubt, must ask the light of the Three Wise Men ... One of the most important goals of Polars is the establishment of contact with the oracle, a group of initiates who are found in the mountains. Thanks to this group, the Polars will in the future be provided with all necessary information in matters of spiritualism and know equally how life on other planets proceeds," – as stated by Zam Bhotiva. To their great regret, the authors were unfortunately not in a position, given their mere esoteric character, in addition to the goals, to also

---

1 Bhotiva, 25 ff.
2 Bhotiva, 145
3 Bhotiva, 146

write down the 12 articles of the statutes of the Polars. Only that much will be revealed: "The articles of the statute confirm ... that the *true* spiritual leaders of the movement of the Polars will be initiates to the highest degree, we almost dare to call them *transhuman,* super-human."[1]

According to Bhotiva, the oracle also transmits longer texts. A 480-word message began, for instance – very gnostizising – with the words: "Man thinks he knows, yet he knows nothing. When he makes progress in knowing, in the realization of the true light, then, unfortunately, he must pass from the world of embodied flesh, since spirit and matter are irreconcileable."[2] "Oh, poor being, why do you torture your Self for dreams and ambitious goals that are always too much? Why all that? You must always die, only to be reborn, and to be reborn, to die again, until you are taken in by the incomprehensible – the return to God. This is the paradise of the various religions." The author points out, that all these oracle messages produce the wonderful impression that we find ourselves in the presence of a center that included all spiritual transmissions of the world. In addition, it provided the sensation that all visions of Katharina Emmerick – the illumination of Saint-Yves d'Alveydre, the teachings of the Lamas and Tibetan Gurus, the Brahmins and the Hindu Yogis – were no dreams.[3]

Many questions to the oracle dealt also with healing methods. Thus, it had been asked for means against malaria and tuberculosis. Against malaria, the content of grapes supposedly helped; against tuberculosis, a respite where the edelweiss blooms.[4] Bhotiva refers to a notation by Prof. Reghini, an outstanding occultist and head of the journal 'Ignis' for initiation studies: "It appears to me that there is a certain relationship between the messages of the oracle and those found by

---

1     Bhotiva, 147 ff.
2     Bhotiva, 50. It is also stated in the oracle's saying that the first pharaoh was a descendent of Atlantis, a son of the sun. [Bhotiva, 51] Stutterheim refers to similar theories in the Bavaria cultural film of 1939 "Germanic People against the Pharaohs," which had been rated by the NS-Censorship as being "educational for people." Stutterheim: "The quintessence of the film is that prior to Egypt's advanced civilization there had been another advanced civilization of Germanic people in the north of Europe, provable and most likely older, and that scientists ought to separate themselves from the purely factual analysis and should consider the supernatural connections." [Stutterheim, 207 ff.] Some columns of the "KdF-Seebad der Zwanzigtausend" (1936-39), a gigantic, 4,5 kilometer long NS-beach-resort in Prora on the island of Rügen, Germany, were built in style of ancient Egypt architecture ( http://www.flickr.com/photos/franzwegener/7082152925 ).
3     Bhotiva, 53 f.
4     Bhotiva, 66 ff.

Saint-Yves d'Alveydre and Ferdinand Ossendowski on the subject of the Three Wise Men ... Both place Three Wise Men at the pinnacle of Agarttha."[1] Bhotiva refers to the various religious transmissions wherein the Three Wise Men are reflected: The Three Wise Men of Atlantis, the three Druids, who had created heaven and the gods, the Magi of the Bible, etc.[2] He claims that Agarttha with its Three Wise Men had inspired certain oracles, like that of Delphi, that of Horus and the "Bel Mardouk," that had dominated the classical world: "... the elevated wise men commanded through the mouths of the various gods, but all carried the symbol of light, the course of history of the classical world, which we are familiar with through the legends and monuments of their people."[3] The secret initiation center was supposedly found also in the excellent summary of René Guénon under the book's title "The King of the World."[4] The existence of a "King of the World" is however denied by the oracle. Upon the question whether he existed, the oracle is claimed to have replied: "Imagination, a crazy idea..."[5] However, the Tibetan wise men behind the oracle fulfilled the expectation for "He, who waits." The Wise Men had stated: "Today, he is still unknown and far away, but tomorrow he will be by the will of the Very-high, be a Great One." Still, in July of 1929, the arrival of this master had been confirmed by the oracle. He would then be *"Commandant Suprême Spirituel des 'Polaires'."*[6]

One of the questioners wanted to know from the oracle where he could find peace. The oracle supposedly replied that he would first need to earn credits by helping the suffering. Then, peace would come to him from the New Light that would be conferred to him from the Anand. Bhotiva said that the Anand mentioned by the oracle referred to the Sanskrit term "ânanda," meaning blessedness. According to the Brahmin-orthodox tradition, the manifestation of the incomprehensible ("Brahma neutre") presented itself under a threefold aspect: 1) Sat (existence), 2) Chit (the total consciousness and 3) Ananda (blessedness). Accordingly, Ananda was said to be the third aspect. A hurried interpretation would find it equal to the Holy Spirit of the Catholic Holy Trinity. But this was not permitted, since their meanings were totally different. It should be noted

---

1   Bhotiva, 74
2   Bhotiva, 66 ff. Guénon: "The name 'Island of Saints' was earlier used for Ireland as the 'green island,' even for England. The island of Helgoland has the same meaning." [Guénon, König, 99]
3   Bhotiva, 89
4   Bhotiva, 79
5   Bhotiva, 84, 86
6   Bhotiva, 94

that this referred to a New Light to come from the Ananda. One could equate Ananda with "He, who waits," whose designation as the Blissful, as the Blessed, was justified.[1]

A Roman occultist, Julius Evola, had directed a long inquiry into the oracle in order to learn the first word on the fifth page of the fifth book in a nearby bookshelf. The answer, which occurred in his presence, supposedly was very simple, saying that this kind of question was totally useless: "And why that?"[2] Julius Evola, one of Mussolini's advisors, had, according to this statement, been in contact with the 'owner of the method' and was familiar with the Polars' method.

René Guénon wrote that he, too, was interested in the oracle, and was to contribute a further article to Zam Bhotiva's work. However, when Bhotiva (Cesare Accomani) and the owner of the oracle technique (Mario Fille) began the foundation of the Polaires, before the oracle had replied to his question, he had separated from Fille and Accomani.[3]

Bhotiva writes about his co-author: "Jean Marquès-Rivière, this young Orientalist and profound authority on Tibet, has in his passionate presentation of the Tibetan initiation rites in 'A l'Ombre des Monastères Thibétains' not only 'materialized' the initiation center, but even localized it in a hidden area, Napamako."[4] And truly, Jean Marquès-Rivière published a book in 1929 by the title "In the Shadow of Tibetan Monasteries." In it he reported of a fictitious journey to Asia. The foreword for it was written by Maurice Magre. He wrote: "In Tibet, it is said, the Wise possess the power to prolong man's life. They are the guardians of the lost, classical knowledge and have, in their archives at their disposal, the history of Atlantis and Lemuria, as well at the future history of mankind, for they have clairvoyance. It is Tibet where this shrouded-in-mystery city of Shambhalla is located, the city of the Wise ..."[5] The novel's hero is initiated by a Buddhist whom he got to know in Paris who led him onto the new path. Marquès-Rivière writes: Before him, everything in me was in doubt, insecure, hopeless. I tried our philosophies, our systems, our religious sects, and increasingly found their great lack of knowledge and total insignificance. Our West is ignorant ... I entered closed circles, the esoteric milieu, the realm of the popes of the occult and did not hear but hollow phrases ... I do not believe that the

---

1     Bhotiva, 124 ff.
2     Bhotiva, 64
3     Guénon, 447-448 (Acc. to Godwin, 89)
4     Bhotiva, 78
5     Magre, Maurice, Foreword, in: Marquès-Rivière, XV

Star of Initiation illuminates the West."¹ Here, belatedly, the autobiographic reference of the novel shows. The novel's hero describes also his initiation: "Following the instructions of the sacred books, I meditated in the lotus position ... I breathed in a special rhythm while I formulated the sacred syllables. Then, I felt the *fire* that arose in me. The snake of initiation, the Kundalini, unrolled from its terrible coil and this tremendous power, the occult source of all magic and the principle of every initiation, awoke ... Through the practices of physical cleansing, my Lama handed me sacred texts for meditation to make my spirit subtle and to form it anew. These were excerpts from the Kangyur, the sacred Tibetan book. This was an enormous collection of 108 volumes of a thousand pages each."² "Lengthy and meticulous breathing exercises and concentration under the supervision of an authorized Lama are necessary ... I then felt my body regularly and literally tremble ... in the higher state, where the spirit is exceptionally lucid, the universe and the concepts of time and space disappear into a deeper unison ..."³ The novel's hero also comments about politics: "One day there will be surprises in the Orient, and the European nations truly play the roles of the cheated and plain instruments in the fingers with their long, well-kept finger nails, cared for by certain Lamas."⁴ "Behind the symbols – the pagodas, the statues, the priests and the Lamas – there are masters, gurus ... who rule Asia, incarnated, living gods, possessing exceptional secrets and a wisdom that is no longer human ... I had earlier the impression, on my journeys in North Africa, especially in Morocco, the south of Arabia, in the Hedyaz and Hasyr, in the face of the spiritual power of Islam ... Following the meetings I had, I believed ... that the occult masters of Islam and Asia's rulers know each other."⁵ He then bemoaned the materialism of the West and praised the spiritualism of the Orient.

But, let us go back to the Star Power Oracle and its authors. To the question of which path led to the legendary realm of Shambhalla, the oracle can advise according to Zam Bhotiva. As one would not expect, the path does not lead via Tibet, but rather one reached the long-since-disappeared, and today possibly underground-located city by means of Moulmein in Burma – according to central Asian tradition. The expert on Tibet, Andreas Gruschke, writes about

---

1 Marquès-Rivière, 24
2 Marquès-Rivière, 34 f.
3 Marquès-Rivière, 37 f.
4 Marquès-Rivière, 134
5 Marquès-Rivière, 147 f.

the realm: "Shambhala is the Sanskrit name of a mythical kingdom, whose geographical location is traditionally given roughly in a far distant and inaccessible region in the northeast of India ... In the transmitted images of the myth, a messianic moment plays a great role for the population: it being that from Shambhala will come the savior of humanity, once when only war [materialism] and destruction ruled in the world." In mythology, it is said about the path to Shambhala: "Whoever, in the search for truth will want to go there without thoughts of return, can achieve it, and obtain that which he is searching for from the master and the wise men of Shambhala." Shambhala is described as follows: "The kingdom of Shambhala is totally surrounded by a circle of snowy mountains, whose glaciers sparkle and glitter. No one who does not belong to this place can pass them ... The snow mountains surrounding the calyx of the lotus have turned entirely into ice cones. They blink and glitter like crystal light. In the interior of the final mountain ring, directly in the center of the kingdom, lies Kapala, the capital of Shambhala. To the east and west of the city lie two very beautiful lakes shaped like a half-moon and a moon sickle, filled with jewels." Gruschke's opinion of Shambhala: "Per the Tibetan tradition the kingdom of Shambhala is part of the so-called 'Hidden Valleys' – certain 'happy valleys,' whose intact world is in times of need available to people with the respective spiritual prerequisites. The importance of the Shambhala realm ... lies less in the possibility of the reality of its geographic location, but rather in the effect of a spiritual quality associated with it."[1]

*"Le leitmotiv symbolique des communications,"* the symbolic leitmotiv of the oracle's transmissions is supposedly based – acording to Bhotiva – on the light of the sun, the sun of the initiated. On this subject the role of the sun should be noted and ascribed to arithmetic by the Katharers. The scientific method of these Initiated was said to be founded on the lessons from the transmissions and rightly so on the arithmetic [numerology], corresponding with the sun.[2] – Referring to the transmissions, the author implies that the Middle Age Katharers had already at their disposal access to the transmissions of the spiritual center – and with that, to the oracle's method. This is also underlined by the reference to the (supposed) importance of numerology for the Katharers. It would also explain the repeated reference of the authors to the "reconstruction" of the the groups of Polars: It would make them a new edition of the *Sapientes*, the wise men of the Katharers. In the light of the intensive occupation of at least one of

---

1     Gruschke, 195 ff.
2     Bhotiva, 58

the authors, Maurice Magre, with the Katharers, this consideration is obvious. The new initiation center in Europe, desired by the Asian center, will therefore develop the Polars in the old Katharic tradition. This would also help to explain a possible expedition of the group to the area of Montségur, of which the Languedoc local press reported. Lange quotes an article of the Toulouse paper *"La Dépeche"* of March 3, 1932: " ... Near Massat, a German [referring to Otto Rahn, who denied this] leads the archaeological work of a group of 'Polaires'. Our readers may remember our report from last summer, in which we reported of the presence of a group of foreign representatives of a theosophical society with a seat in Paris (Avenue Rapp) in the upper Ariège: the 'Polaires' ... What then did the 'Polaires' do last summer in the Ariège? As we described already, it deals with the archaeological excavation at castle Montségur – whose goal it is to raise to the light of day the treasures of the Albigensians, which, in the 13th century, were assumed to have been left in the fortification and caves. ..." However, there are also unconfirmed sources, following which not Montségur, but the Katharer castle Lordat had been the goal of the Polaires expedition in 1931.[1]

---

1   Citing Lange, Rahn, 36 f. – With reference to the Polars, the article was four days later disclaimed by Otto Rahn in the form of a reader's letter on March 7, 1932. The disclaimer refers however only to his person, not on the evidently earlier report of the paper about the visit of Polaires on Montségur. Acc. to Colum Hayward the journey of the Polaires to Lordat in the Pyrenees took place in July of 1931 upon the direction of the oracle, there to find an Albigenser treasure which was, however, not found. [Cooke, 26, 34, 48, 118 – since the source itself originates from the esoteric milieu and I do not have the opportunity to question Cooke's statements, or Hayward's, respectively as to their sources, these statements can be enjoyed only with great reservation!] Cooke names as seat of the Polars: Avenue Junot, No. 36, 18e, on the western slope of the Montmatre, Paris. [Cooke, 65, 218] Castle Lordat is located 13 kilometers from Montségur. Following the tragedy of Montségur, it supposedly served as a Katharer refuge. [ http://www.cathares. org/lordat-intro.html ] With Cooke is found information about a supposed branch of the Polars in England. Zam Bhotiva supposedly established the contact between Paris and London. Hayward writes to it: "Their main office [of the Polaris Brotherhood] was in Paris, from where it operated from 1926 (as far as is known to us) until the time of occupation ... 1934, a branch was founded in England which, soon separated from the French organization and from which in the year 1936 the White Eagle Lodge arose." [Cooke, 13; http://www.whiteeagle.de ] "From where the Polaires took their name and why they chose the symbol of the six-pointed star that adorned the cover page of their magazine, no exact information is available. It was only said that the Polair oracle had given the instruction to use the star: ... 'as a collective signal for the erring-about, the run-aground, and those found in darkness.' At another place the small star the Polaires wore, was describes as a replica of the larger star ... – Bulletin, May 9, 1930, page 3" [Cooke, 16] A dead Indian, called "White Eagle," supposedly announced the medium

Yet, Jean Marquès-Rivière was later to play an important role in the de-

Grace Cooke, called "Minesta," wife of Ivan Cooke, that a contact with an organization in France would come to pass. The Polaires again had learned from their oracle that the dead Sir Arthur Conan Doyle, author of "Sherlock Holmes," would speak via a medium. Thus, it had also been published in the bulletin January-March 1931. Then, a messenger of the Polars had truly appeared in England: Zam Bhotiva. [Cooke, 19 f.] It came to a common gathering. The participants were supposedly the widow of Sir Conan Doyle, Lady Doyle, "as well as Zam Bhotiva and the 'Head' of the Polaires, we are familiar with by the name of 'R. Odin.' (He may not be mistaken with Mario Fille, the 'Wise,' who knew the password and established the actual connection with the Hermit of Bagnia.)" [Cooke, 22] Ivan Cooke, spouse of the medium, through which her dead husband had spoken, had supposedly written to Lady Doyle in 1932: "Please thank White Eagle for his comforting message. It is good to know that a group of such wonderful, dear people as you have been selected for the great center." [cited after Cooke, 25] It is said that in 1931 the Englishmen, on their way to the Pyrenees, were first initiated in Paris. [Cooke, 27] Instead of the Katharers' treasure an immaterial treasure had been discovered: "Even the medium [Minesta] began to realize only ten years later what actually had happened in Lordat and what had been at the root of this expedition. The said treasure was only a totally immaterial and spiritual treasure ... It lay in the aura emanating from saintly brothers of the sacred mountain; from St. John himself, if one so wishes. During the ten days of their stay in Lordat Minesta had totally taken in by this aura, her soul had become totally been absorbed in it. So, Brighteyes [Minesta] had truly found the promised treasure. She carried it inside herself when she left Lordat." [Cooke, 35] In 1934 a Polaire lodge was established in London following Bhotiva's instructions. Bhotiva supposedly consecrated it. But there had also been problems: "On recommendation of Bhotiva's a member of the Paris Polaires living in London was allowed to join the English brotherhood. But there were personal discrepancies, not to be entered into here more closely. She was finally advised to leave. Because of connected resignations, Bhotiva was asked for advice. He suggested to appoint the person who had been discharged as the head of the English Polaires, thus bringing the English group under the immediate supervision of Paris. The suggestion was inevitably rejected. On advice of White Eagle the English group broke all connections with the French group at the beginning of the following year [1936]." [Cooke, 29] Hayward writes to the development of the Paris Polaires: "Increasingly, occult subjects were treated in the Bulletins, a process symbolically confirmed in January of 1933 with the renaming in *Les Cahiers* – Notebooks. But what happened of the planned social plans of the Polaires? A forum for occult ideas? Or did they wait only for the instructions of the 'The one waiting?' ... The exact time, 1933 or 1934 ... was, as has been said, unusual ... The Polaires considered the coming master as Hyperborean (even Aryan) ... What then happened, leads us ever deeper into the area of guessing ... [A collaborator of Zam Bhotiva's publishing house] told us that the author visited the business at the beginning of the fifties and had explained that the Polaires in France had come to an end. When the English group separated in 1935, a small remaining rest of the English Polaires maintained the connection with the French group. Until a few years ago they had faithfully met." [Cooke, 31 f.] Zam Bhotiva supposedly quit the Polaires

struction of the French secret organizations in that part of France occupied by Germany. As one can see from his above evaluation of the secret organizations, he did this not from a misunderstood missionary eagerness as an accomplice of enlightenment and rationality, but possibly because the activities of these organizations did not appear to him sufficiently spiritual. Following the German occupation of France's north in 1940, a special police to fight the Freemasons was established on Dec. 15, 1941 by decree of the interior ministry for the two French zones (occupied and free North and Vichy). The service employed 300 agents in 1944 for the north and south.[1] Marquès-Rivière was nominated head of this police for the north.[2] In mid-1943, he directed the division for investigation in the *Service des Sociétés Secretès Z.O.*, also the *Zone occupée*, the occupied zone.[3] He was obviously paid directly by the Germans.[4] This political police, abbreviated S.S.S., had the assignment to destroy France's secret organizations.[5] Its headquarters for the occupied zone was in Paris in the requisitioned house of the Theosophical Society, 4, Square Rapp, Paris. The establishment of the S.S.S. took place under German control of the Gestapo-SD-Lieutenant Moritz.[6] The Vichy Regime in the south of France, collaborating with the Nazis, had also a S.S.S., which occupied itself with the same task in the service of the Gestapo. Both cooperated. Assignments, e.g. for the French Rotary Club, arrived directly from Germany to the desk of the S.S.S.[7] How irrationally Marquès-Rivière operated is demonstrated by his efforts to discover the archives of the Freemasons by means of French city maps and with the help of a radio-aesthetic.[8] Most likely the archival locations were to be tracked down by pendulum – at the time, the classic operation for such tasks in occult circles. Marquès-Rivière forwarded results of his S.S.S. work directly to the Germans. In general, important documents from the Freemason archives were to be forwarded to the SD in Berlin, unimportant

---

    and thus opened the way for Mario Fille who, in 1936 supposedly lead separate groups of women and men of the Polars in Paris, Geneva, New York, and Belgrade. (*Cahiers de la Fraternité Polaire,* n.s., 1, March-April 1936 (acc.to Godwin, 91; unfortunately, I was unable to access the copy bibliographically.)

1    Sabah, 510
2    Sabah, 434 f.
3    Sabah, 480
4    Sabah, 275
5    A 1942 order of Himmler's for the destruction of Polish secret organizations is known. [Himmler, Dienstkalender, 401, footnote 44]
6    Sabah, 177. In 1942 the Gestapo also directed the S.S.S. in the Z.O.. [Sabah, 439]
7    Sabah, 176
8    Sabah, 28, 337

documents were to be sent to the director of the National Library, Bernard Faÿ.[1] Documents and books of this nature, from other occupied countries, were, as a rule, stored in the Central Library of the Reich-Security-Headquarters in Berlin-Wilmersdorf in the former lodge house used by the SD in Emserstr. 12.[2] Two listings of the members of the French Freemasons were also forwarded to the Germans by the S.S.S. They might have contained about 60,000 names. 549 of these Freemasons were executed, 989 were deported.[3] The basic motivation for this activity was presented by Marquès-Rivière as follows: "Once we are a generation further, Freemasonry will become a widow without children and disappear in the grave of extinct religions and rites. There remains its provider of ideas and its employer –, the Jew … without Freemasonry he will lose many of his means."[4] Marquès-Rivière also pursued public relations, such as the organization of, among other things, an anti-Freemasonry exhibition in Nancy.[5] In 1946, several S.S.S.-collaborators were taken to court. Bernard Faÿ, professor at the Collège de France and head administrator of the Bibliothèque Nationale was, for instance, sentenced to a lifetime of forced labor for his denunciation of French Freemasons. Jean Marquès-Rivière was able to flee in time.[6] He was sentenced to death in absentia.[7]

---

1 Sabah, 436
2 Schroeder, Werner, article: "Die Bibiotheken des RSHA: Aufbau und Verbleib," Print copy of the lecture, held in Weimar on September 11, 2003 at the conference "Provenienzforschung für die Praxis. Recherche und Dokumentation von Provenienzen in Bibliotheken," Page 5 – Acc. to the progress report of Office VII, the establishment of a Library of Secret Sciences (Theosophy, Occultism, etc.) (which did not just include Freemasonry and the occult) from the plundered holdings was begun. This demonstrates that no destruction of the collected knowledge in book form was intended – no incineration took place, but for the option of later utilization of the material. In 1943 at least 250,000 not yet evacuated volumes were destroyed in an air raid on the former lodge house. Schroeder showed as balance: "After 11 years of activity the librarians of the Central Library of the RSHA had gathered a total of about two to three million volumes, foremost plunder, of which 400- to 500,000 volumes survived the war." [ http://www.initiativefortbildung.de/pdf/provenienz_schroeder.pdf ]
3 Sabah, 175, 337
4 Marquès-Rivière, citing Sabah, 176
5 Sabah, 439
6 Sabah, 337 f. The kind of suffering a Frenchman would incur getting into the apparatus of the S.S.S., Argus demonstrates by the example of residents of Villeneuve-sur-Lot. [Argus (pseud.): *"Contribution à l'histoire des Francs-Maçons sous l'occuption,"* Chiré-en-Montreuil 1988, 192 f. (after Sabah, 336)]
7 Trimondi, 287

Are there signs that the SS knew of the bizarre ideas of the Polars?

In July of 1937, SS-Brigade-Leader Wiligut received a letter of de Mengel's. He reported to the head of Himmler's personal staff: "In a highly secretive-kept letter of June 23, '37, Mr. Gaston de Mengel conveyed a most peculiar message to me. He writes something like the following: 'The axis located northeast of Paris works very well. However, the axis lies neither near Berlin nor Helsinki. I have from the average of the axis been able to determine the point of departure of the forces. It lies in Murm (Lapland) about 35 degrees eastern longitude and 68 degrees northern latitude in the surroundings of the Lowosero in Russia. I have also determined the location of the great Black-Center. It is located within the great triangle formed by Kobdo, Urumtshi and Bakul, near Sin-kinag in western Mongolia'. I bring this letter to your attention, since Gaston de Mengel asked me what I thought of it. I think this information to be notable and request your respective attention. According to my assumption, the Russians with agreement of France and England are establishing aircraft bases there. Whether this assumption is correct, the SD [the SS-Security Service] could try to find out." The letter was listed as "secret!"[1]

In 1934, Günther Kirchhoff (1892-1975) of Gaggenau near Baden-Baden, who was interested in Germanic history, entered Himmler's catchment area. He posited the theory of the existence of geodesic energy lines covering entire continents.[2] Today, this occult approach functions to my knowledge under the name of geomancy. Wiligut, too, was a follower of these ideas. In this context, he made an official SS-trip to Gaggenau, prior to de Mengel's visit to Berlin in 1936. Summarizing, he subsequently wrote: "Comparing the location systems I found (based on the Irmins belief) and that of Mr. Kirchhoff, it turned out that the system found by me diverges by 2 degrees east against the north-south direction. Mr. Günther Kirchhoff has, based on the numerous extant cultural sites, etc., found that this location lines are up to 46 degrees oriented to the west (from the north-south direction); from this it can be concluded that, considering the old cult places, a multiple shift of the earth axis can be demonstrated."[3] Guénon called this activity area – as explained above – "Sacred Geography."[4] Wiligut also went further back to the location theories of the Extern-Stones

---

1    Germ. Fed. Arch, NS 19, 3974, page 45
2    Germ. Fed. Arch, NS 21/31, Kirchhoff letter of June 14, 1934 to Weisthor; Goodrick-Clarke, 184 ff., 259
3    Citing Lange, Wiligut, 185
4    Guènon, König, 36

c / Akmerts / de Mengel

Übersetzung des Briefes von Herrn G. de Mengel vom 2.Juli 1937

...... Ich schrieb an Brigadeführer Weisthor,um ihm über das Resultat der verschiedenen Erfahrung,die ich bei meiner Reise Paris-Berlin-Helsinki sammeln konnte,Rechenschaft abzulegen. Bei gleicher Gelegenheit sandte ich einen ähnlichen Bericht an meinen russischen Freund in Paris und erhielt von ihm vor einigen Tagen als Antwort einige Auskünfte,die ich aus dem Russischen übersetzen und Ihnen mitteilen will. Seien Sie bitte so freundlich dies ins Deutsche zu übersetzen und reichen Sie es an Brigadeführer Weisthor weiter, dem ich mit gleicher Post schreibe und die einzelnen Namen,die ich im vorliegenden Schreiben durch Buchstaben ersetze,ohne Erklärung schicke.

Vor einigen Jahren erhielt mein russischer Freund ( er half uns 1933 im Kampfe gegen Oung Mong, und war so verwegen,uns unter folgenschen Vorwänden zu schreiben) aus Cuba ein Paket mit von Oung Mong herrührenden Dokumenten,welche dazu dienen sollten,sogenannte "Buddhistische Zentren in verschiedenen Ländern zu gründen. In der Anlage seines Briefes,der mich vor einigen Tagen erreichte,schickte er mir eine Zusammenfassung eines dieser Dokumente.

Auszug einer von Oung Mong 1934 veröffentlichten Erklärung.

Das geheime Hauptzentrum der ganzen buddhistischen Welt,das unter dem Namen "Einsiedlerreich der Welt",ist,wie man behauptet,zerschlagen Ch'An Cheng Cob" bekannt ist,ist,wie man behauptet,zerschlagen worden. Nichts ist falscher als dies. Es ist nur an einen sichereren Ort verlegt worden,weil da,wo es früher lag,in Urumchi in Sin-Kiang die politischen Konflikte und andere Unruhen das Führen unseres heiligen Sitzes "Päpstlicher Stuhl" an diesen Orte unmöglich machten. Vor kurzem ist das "Einsiedlerreich der Welt" "Momache" geworden und hat sich augenblicklich am Thibet niedergelassen.

...... Man hat in der Welt sich widersprechende und irrige Kommentare verbreitet,die von einer schlecht unterrichteten Presse sowie von Gesellschaften,die der Gegenwart des erwarteten Messias in dieser Welt,des neuen Belehrers der Welt,des Herrn Maitreya,von dem man annimmt,er sei die letzte Reinkarnation des Buddha,nicht freundlich gegenüb rstehen,herrühren; man versichert schliesslich,dass er (Maitreya?) der Prior des buddhistischen Zentrums von Ch'An Cheng Cob,das in Asien mehr unter dem Namen von Mutulku Krug

- 2 -

Hsih und in der ganzen Welt bis vor kurzem unter "Ehrwürdiger (Meister vom Stuhl) Anagarika Chasshekarkrayn alias Oung Mong, Cherenski usw., bekannt ist,bei.

Dieses Dokument bestätigt das Ergebnis meiner Erfahrungen und ebenso unsere Ansicht,dass Oung Mong wenn nicht der oberste Chef des "Zentrums der Schwarzen" so doch wenigstens einer seiner Hauptbeauftragten ist. Der Autor dieses Dokuments hat das "Grosse Zentrum der Weissen",das "Agharta" (mongolisch Aghartî) sei,er schickt,den Eindruck zu erwecken,dass dieses Zentrum das "Grosse gibt ihm zu diesem Zweck den gleichen Namen und macht die,die evtl. die Gelegenheit bezweifeln könnten,glauben,dass es sich nicht mehr an diesem Platz befinde ( während es noch immer dort ist). Er kann jedoch die,die wissen,dass das Agharta Zentrum durch Zufall hereingeriet,er niemals widerkäme,nicht täuschen. Vor einigen Jahren haben die Engländer zu diesem Versuch eine irrsinnige Summe (im Umkreis von 1500 km von Schwarzen ist,dass seine Sonne Lage (im Umkreis von 1500 km von Schwarzen Zentrum entfernt) und sein Eingang für alle,ausgenommen die,die das Recht des Eintritts besitzen,unauffindbar ist,dass,wenn jemand durch Zufall hereingeriet,er niemals widerkäme,nicht täuschen. ausgegeben.

Seien Sie weiter so freundlich,die einzelnen folgenden Mitteilungen,die ich von einer irländischen Dame,mit der ich einige Mal sprach,erhielt,weiterzugeben.

Die Atmosphäre in Paris ist unruhiger als je zuvor und die sowjetrussischen Einflüsse machen sich immer mehr im Volke bemerkbar, es ist über die während der Präsidentschaft Blums erhaltenen Konzessionen ärgerlich und wird immer unzufriedener,weil das Leben teurer geworden und es viel mehr für Gas und Transport bezahlen muss. Die jüdischen Elemente werden immer aktiver. Ein Neffe des Neville Chamberlain,Howard Chamberlain,hat sich kürzlich zum Judentum bekehrt und scheint mit den sowjetistischen Juden von Moskau in Verbindung zu stehen; er macht eine ausserordentliche Propaganda unter der Volksfront,hat zahlreiche Broschüren geschrieben; in einigen von diesen stellt er die Behauptung auf,die Bewohner der britischen Inseln sind selbst von Irland seien Nachkommen von Juden. Denen,die die gälische Sprache und Mythologie kennen,sind seine Argumente absurd,dennoch haben diese Broschüren einen gefährlichen Einfluss auf die Ignoranten.

Translation of de Mengels communication about the "Zentrum der Schwarzen" (Center of the Blacks) through the "Ahnenerbe der SS" (Ancestral Inheritance) (German Federal Archives / Bundesarchiv)

researcher, Wilhelm Teudt.[1] De Mengel has, following the applied subject names and the aid of geomancy methods, determined the location as the "Black-Center."

On July 2, 1937, another letter of de Mengel's arrived. It's translation reads:

"A few years ago, my Russian friend (he assisted us in 1933 in the fight against the Oung Mong, and was daring enough to write to us under a false name) received a parcel from Cuba holding Oung Mong-originating documents, meant to serve the founding of so-called 'Buddhist Centers' in different countries. Attached to his letter I received a few days ago, he sent to me a summary of one of the documents.

Excerpt of an Oung Mong declaration published in 1934

The secret main center of the entire Buddhist world, known by the name of 'Hermit Realm of the World' and as the 'Buddhist Center Ch'An Cheng Cob,' has been, as is claimed, destroyed. Nothing is more false than this. It has only been relocated to a safer place, since where it was earlier, in Urumchi in Sin-Kiang, the political conflicts and other disturbances made the leading of our sacred seat 'Pontifical Seat' impossible. Recently, the 'Hermit Realm of the World' has become 'Nomad' and has settled for the time being in Tibet ..... Contradictory and erroneous comments have been spread throughout the world, originating from a poorly informed press as well as societies, whose position is not friendly towards the presence of the expected messiah to this world. He is the new teacher of the world, the Lord Maitreya, who is thought to be the last reincarnation of Buddha. Finally, it has been assured that he is (Maitreya?), the prior of the Buddhist Center of Ch'an Cheng Cob, better known in Asia by the name of Hutulktu Krang Hsi, and in the entire world until recently as Honorable (Master of the Chair) Anagarika Chasshekankrakrya aka Oung Mong, Cherenski, etc..

This document confirms the result of my experiences as well as our [!] viewpoint that Oung Mong, if not the topmost chief of the 'Center of Blacks', then is at least one of its main designates. The author of this document has the talent to give the impression that this center is supposed to be the 'Great Center of the Wise Men', the 'Agarttha' (Mongolian Agharti), and for this purpose is giving it

---

1   Lange, Wiligut, 60, 131. Lange: "When in May of 1945, at St. Quirin at the Tegernsee, American and British soldiers seized Himmler's private papers and books, a typewritten manuscript 'Der Asen Ursprung und Wirkung' of Günther Kirchhoff was found among them" [Lange, Wiligut, 299] To Wilhelm Teudt (1860-1942) also: Mohler, I., 347

the same name and makes those, who might doubt the situation believe, think that it is no longer at this place (while it is still there). However, he cannot deceive those who know that Aghartta is secret, that its precise location (in the vicinity of 1,500 km distant from the black center) and its entrance, except for those with the right of entry, is untraceable, and that anyone entering it by accident would never return. Several years ago, the English spent an insane amount in an unsuccessful attempt."[1]

We are talking then of a "Center of the Blacks," whose head or at least its "Chief designate" is said to be Anagarika, aka Oung Mong, or also Cherenski. Who could this "Cherenski" mentioned here be? By name, a similar sounding gentleman, supposedly also involved in occult connections, is mentioned in Heise's book about "Occult Lodges," which Himmler read in 1926. It concerns the Jewish-Russian minister of revolution Alexander Kerenski (1881-1970). Kerenski was Russian War and Justice Minister following the Tsar's deposition and fled to Paris after the October Revolution where he published an émigré paper in 1922-32. He wrote numerous studies about the Russian revolution. When the Germans entered Paris in 1940, he fled again, this time to the USA.[2] Heise mentions Kerenski as a member of a Jewish order, meaning the "Jewish obscure-religious Bnai Brith Order." Kerenski is said to be "the Russian attorney and revolution minister Karbis (adopted as ‚Kerenski')." Heise writes: "It is absolutely true what Rudolf von Sebottendorf says in the 'Magical Leaves' (June-July 1920), that 'Bolshevism is logically the extreme consequence and final result of the Romance (i.e. British) political Masonry ... Concerning 'Br.' Kerenski (Karbis), the Russian General Plowzoff openly said in 'Echo de Paris' that this former minister of revolution and special friend of England's and the British Violence Lodge is a 'protector of Bolshevism'."[3] Heise continues in his comments about the Russian revolution and its protagonists: "It touches us occultists oddly, but it confirms anew the inner connection between dark-magic lodges and politics, and that it was Trotsky, who ... found for himself and his Soviet 'brothers' the pleasure of a so-called 'Black Mass' or Mason 'satanic liturgy', wherein the 'field captain of the dark crowds' was gratefully paid tribute to for the completed revolution ... This Black Mass is simultaneously the vivid illustration for the fine occult 'good nose', by which the Russian wenches in the fellowship of the despots Lenin and Trotsky were 'made ready'. Special means

---

1     Germ. Fed. Arch, NS 19, 3974, page 48 f.
2     http://www.dhm.de/lemo/html/biografien/KerenskiAlexander/
3     Heise, 65

awaken in these eastern suffragettes a particular kind of inner perception for the Fluidum, streaming from the young and older warrior blood of killed ‚enemies' ... where after the Megaeres are loosened ... onto all armed or unarmed opponents of Leninesque tyrannis, – and these thus ‚tenderly sensitive-made' disgusting Amazons now taste the blood, before they have made it liquid from their occult bloodlust and throw themselves ... onto the ... young and old male victims."[1] As a reminder: Himmler commented on Heise's book with the words: "A deeply serious text that suggests much. There is a good and a bad principle, acting and manifesting itself in human society."[2] In any case, Kerenski fit into the dualistic picture of black and white magicians said to fight for world supremacy. Whether de Mengel really means Kerenski here, when he writes Cherenski, must, however, remain open – despite being highly plausible.

It is highly probable that de Mengel truly declares here the former Russian minister the occult mastermind, for Johann Strunk, of Ludendorff's milieu, one year after de Mengel's letter to Wiligut/Himmler, in 1938 drew a connecting line between the occult powers in Tibet and the Russian minister: "The overthrow of the tsar empire is foremost the deed of Jews, Freemasons, and Jesuits, in which they were supported by the occultists, most likely often unintentionally. The transitional government, subsequent to Lwoff's ministry, was formed by the Jew Kerenski. Whether he was in the service of the Eastern Priesthood is difficult to decide. However, the swastica, Lama priests liked to misuse on protective amulets for their secret actions, appearing on the rubel bills issued by his government, makes one wonder."[3]

The translation of de Mengel's expositions is commented on Aug. 19, 1937, in a letter to the SS-Untersturmführer Kurt Ruppmann of the SS-Reichsführer's personal staff by Grönhagen's secretary Gertraut Schlarb: "My entirely private opinion of it is that a great portion of pompous behavior wrote this, for the opposite side will not see the Reichsführer as quite such an idiot and avail itself of such clumsily stupid things in order to set him on the wrong track [!]. De Mengel has a strong inclination for mysticism; he has surely experienced much and has mixed here facts with fantasy. Furthermore, one must consider that he is over 60 years old and therefore tends toward one-sidedness. As to the subject itself: Do you believe that an organization intent on working in secret, will select an isolated place as described here, only to be observed at every congress

---

1    Heise, 66
2    Himmler, Reading list, Page 39, Title no. 258, read in February of 1926
3    Strunk, 50

c/ de Mengel    eing. 29.6.
                Nr. 468.

                        Gaston de MENGEL
                        Urheikukatu 16. c. 51.
23 June 1937            Helsinki

Lieber Herr Weisthor,

Sie wissen vermutlich durch Fraulein Schlark dass Ich bin mit meinem Anfang in Finnland ganz und gar zufrieden.

Nun, schreibe Ich über eine Sache die wird wahrscheinlich Ihr Interesse erregen.

Vorgestern hat Man durch die Achse, die von Paris liegt N.O., sehr stark arbeiten. Aber, da liegt die Richtung dieser Achse nicht von Berlin oder von Helsinki dieselben genau, Ich habe uns ihren Durchschnitt den Ausgangspunkte die kräfte bestimmen können: er liegt in Murm (Lappland), etwa 35° long. O x 60° cat. N. in Umgebungen Lowosero, das Russland zugehört. Gleich habe Ich den Ort von den grossen Schwartzzentrum bestimmen: er liegt innerhalb der Dreieck das Kobdo, Urumtsi und Baikal bilden in Sin-kiang (N. Mongolei). Was denken Sie davon?

Mit herzlichen Grüssen
G. de Mengel

Letter de Mengels to Karl-Maria Wiligut (aka Weisthor), Himmler's occult advisor, 1937, concerning the „grossen Schwartzzentrum" ("great Black-Center")
(Germ. Fed. Arch. / Bundesarchiv)

by so-and-so-many detectives? Is this not more advantageous in a large city? In addition, the reports are such that one cannot take anything from them that would be of importance to the SD. But you will see for yourself what there is in this matter."[1]

Himmler's house and home occultist, the force field locator Wiligut, obviously cannot make sense of the "most secretly kept letter" of de Mengel's. The secretary, who translated de Mengel's oeuvre, obviously cannot either, since she doubts de Mengel's mental condition ("fantasy") and suggests age dementia ("over 60 years old") However, de Mengel would hardly write such a letter and send it to the SS if he were not of the opinion that there would be a recipient able to understand the message. It would appear that it meant for Himmler himself, for what other addressee could a letter to SS-Brigade-Leader Wiligut, Himmler's confidant in matters of the occult, have aside from Wiligut himself? Furthermore, Schlarb implies Himmler's attention regarding de Mengel's messages, or she would not write that the opposite side would not supply Himmler with such clumsy misinformation (to suggest the real Black Center as the Aghartta of the Wise Men), in order to "put him on the wrong track" – For this to happen, Himmler truly has to receive the information. Beyond this, Schlarb doubts here only the tactic presented by de Mengel, but not at all the existence of the "opposite side," meaning the lord of the Black-Center. Since Himmler was clearly the intended recipient of the letter, it is possible to conclude from it some of the contents of the conversation of Himmler-de Mengel, for in this conversation the circumstances must have been cleared up, whose knowledge was the prerequisite for the understanding of de Mengel's actual message. With this, the transfer of ideas between a coworker or even member of the Polaires and Himmler is proved.

---

1   Germ. Fed. Arch., NS 19, 3974, page 47. Two years later, on June 21, 1939, the SS-Obersturmführer Ruppmann sent a letter to the head of the SS-Reichsführer's personal staff, SS-Gruppenführer Wolff. This letter states: "Attached, please find documentation on the research of Mr. De Mengel. Following a suggestion of Mr. Colonel Weißthor, the SS-Reichsführer has ordered that the total of the so named are to be photocopied. These photocopies are presently still kept in a safe in the house on Kaspar-Theystr. 33. I have already spoken about this with SS-Sturmbannführer Sievers. He has no use for these documents. I thought already to send the material to Colonel Wiligut for him to deal with. However, its processing on his part is not possible since the notes are written in French language and the Mr. Colonel does not know this language. Possibly the Wewelsburg has use for it? I request a decision what to do with this material." [Germ. Fed. Arch.NS 19, 3974, page 1] Only the German-language compilation of Gaston de Mengel's writings and the file concerning the letter correspondence have been preserved.

In order to understand the message, at least in part, we must once more briefly address the Polars and their oracle. One of the antagonists of the Good with Bhotiva is the Kala-Nag, the Black Snake. With the Esoterics it is supposedly preferentially treated – according to Bhotiva – as the symbol of an evil power. In a dialog with the oracle, it appeared rather as the essence of a physical plan: The probable leader of a sect of the Black Magicians, is the turned-opposite hypostase of a higher being.[1] This sect or group had magical means at its disposal, just as powerful as those of the White Initiates.[2] The Polar Zam Bhotiva imagines here a sect that can take on the Tibetan Initiation Center of the Wise Men, the members of the White Lodge: the Black Magicians. One may imply that they agitate as the antipodes of the White Lodge from a "Black" Center. This center would then have, analogous to the White Men in Tibet, at least one leader, the Head of the Black Magicians.

When de Mengel writes: "I have also determined the location of the great Black Center," he by no means refers to some kind of military base, as Wiligut obviously fantasizes short of any introduction into the secrets of the French occult scene, but the "Center of the Blacks," as it is called in the second letter. And, as he established, the "highest chief" of this center acts as the chief of the Black Magicians. That this deals truly with the dualistic theology, found also with the Polars, shows de Mengel's reference to the "'Great Center of the Wise Men', this being 'Aghartta' ... ." Besides, Himmler was familiar with the basics of the idea of a secret initiation center from his readings of Ossendowski's "Animals, Humans, and Gods."

At this point, a reminder of de Mengel's article about the Freemasons is necessary. He, too, sensed a worldwide conspiracy of dark forces: "We cannot repeat it often enough: The speculative Freemasonry, like Judaism, like theosophy ... likewise the political movements, national or global, be they ever so contradictory, are all nothing but instruments, manipulated by groups equipped with an undreamed-of power that aims for a singular and terrible goal ..."[3] An assessment of the situation that connected him with Zam Bhotiva and also Heise. That this assessment was not at all uncommon at the time, is demonstrated by a look at the life and work of Rudolf Steiner's. His biographer, Christoph Lindenberg, writes: "Sometime after August 20, 1914, Rudolf Steiner received

---

1 Bhotiva, 118. The Munich gnostic, Alfred Schuler, inspired by Papus, saw the world threatened by the Black Magus. [Wegener, Schuler, 138 f.]
2 Bhotiva, 128
3 Mengel, Infidelité, 323 f.

the message that Generaloberst Helmuth von Moltke, the Head of the German General Staff, would like to see him. Since 1904 Steiner was acquainted with Mrs. Eliza von Moltke, and although Helmuth von Moltke did not share the spiritualistic inclinations of his wife – he had gained trust in Rudolf Steiner and his spiritualistic direction and had even read some of it."[1] "In December of 1916 and January 1917, Rudolf Steiner lectured once more in Dornach about the world-historical situation and the causes of the World War … On the basis of this rich knowledge [among others, the study of several "meters of literature about the outbreak of the World War"], Steiner delivered a total of 25 speeches about the events of the time and complemented a number of facts by referrals to the occult connections underlying them …" Among other things he spoke of the activities of occult brotherhoods.[2] Lindenberg continues: "As an insight from Moltke's post-human life [Moltke had already died in 1916] Rudolf Steiner conveyed in 1921: 'It was not possible to get through in September of 1914 …' Two years later it says from the same source …: 'we were totally forsaken by the gods. We left ourselves to the activities of ghosts, of which one pulled in this direction, the other in the opposite. All of Europe was subject to this activity … To this were added the others, which had allied themselves at the Weichsel with the Oriental demons. All this impacted the souls. One cannot do anything else but what has happened.'"[3] Thus, Steiner similarly agreed with Heise's view, as read by Himmler, that the outbreak of the World War had come to pass because of the influence of spirits, demons, as well as occult brotherhoods. Similar to the presentation of the dead British military man, Nelson, appears the deceased Moltke with Heise. The similarity of Steiner's ideas with those of Heise are not accidental. Lindenberg points out that Heise's conspiratory-theoretical text, preceded the "Occult Lodges," read by Himmler and in its content is almost identical: "The Entente-Freemasonry and the World War" was suggested by Steiner's lectures 1916/1917 and was even financed by Steiner with 3,600 sfr, the "Printing Charges" – as Steiner wrote.[4] – As absurd as the thought of control

---

1  Lindenberg, Biography, II, 572
2  Lindenberg, Biography, II, 582-584
3  Lindenberg, Biography, II, 586
4  Lindenberg, Chronicles, 392: "January 19, [1918]. Letter to Emma Boos-Jegher, with which Rudolf Steiner said that it had been possible to provide Heise with the 'sum for printing' (sfr 3,600) for his book Die Entente-Freimaurerei und der Weltkrieg. Mrs. Boos-Jegher had established the connection with the publisher. Based on Rudolf Steiners contemporary historical lectures from winter 1916/17, Heise had treated the subject."

of political events by supra-natural forces appears to us today, as widespread do they seem to have been in occult circles at the time.

In the light of Himmler's lasting enthusiasm for spiritualism, his affinity for the Katharers, his promotion of the occultist (Wiligut), released from an insane asylum, his knowledge of Ossendowski's remarks about the initiation center in the Himalayas[1] and his positive recognition of Heise's comments about the

---

1   In 1938/39 an expedition to Tibet took place under the patronage of the SS-Reichsführer. [Detailed information to the Tibet Expedition may be found with Kater, 212 ff., with Greve, Reinhard, article: "Tibetforschung im SS-Ahnenerbe," in: Hauschild, 168 ff. and with Hale, Christopher: "Himmler's Crusade: The true story of the 1938 Nazi expedition to Tibet," London 2003.] Greve: "Beger transferred also the philological processing of the Tibetan stamps and coins to Schubert. It is assumed that Schubert worked also with the unpublished works of the Tibet scholar, A. Grünwedel, which was kept in a special Ahnenerbe-department under the leadership of W. Wüst." [Hauschild, 193 ]] Their utilization took years. As of April 1944, a work study of the "Lehr- und Forschungsstätte für Innerasien und Expeditionen, Mittersill, Salzburgerland" about the final four months is available. In it it states: "3rd Dept. Geophysics – SS-Obersturmführer (F) Wienert completed his habilitation. It demonstrated outstanding physical results about the Tibetan plateau. Furthermore, Wienert was occupied with secret special tasks he had been assigned with by the SS-Standardführer Sievers ..." [Germ. Fed. Arch.NS 19, 2709, page 92] Whether the here mentioned secret special tasks of the geologist, Karl Wienert, dealt also with the clarification of esoterically motivated, possibly geomansic questions, like the search for occult centers, we do not know. The fact is that race-related medical tests were conducted on Tibetan people. In 1929, the later Nazi-collaborator and Tibet specialist, Marquès-Rivière, had reported in his book about an initiation center and its ruler in Tibet: "[Der Herr der drei Welten. – [Die drei Welten: Hölle, Erde und Wohnsitz der Götter. [Marquès-Rivière, 195]]] was not always in Napamakou. Tradition tells us that the mighty lord ruled before the renowned Lhasa dynasty ... in the West, on a mountain range surrounded by large forests ... At that time there was still a flower on the swastika. But the black time circles drove off the Lord of the West which is how He came to the Orient ... Once a year He issues his orders to his people and the peoples of Asia via an ambassador of his kingdom, who visits Lhasa." [Marquès-Rivière, 137 f.] This ambassador of the secret center [Marquès-Rivière, 187] is described of being a nordic type: "His facial features appear young, his temples, however, white. His skin is light and I could easily differentiate a purely caucasian type from the background of the brownish, wrinkled faces of the crowd surrounding him." [Marquès-Rivière, 139] It is therefore unlikely that the race-medical tests of the populace, were motivated by rumors from the occult camp about final nordic rulers in Tibet. The results of the measuring are different: The part of nordic racial features within the Tibetan populace was percentagewise expressed minimal – very different from the Indians listed also by the expedition, who had a clearly greater similarity with Europeans. [See: Greve, Reinhard, Article: "Tibetforschung im SS-Ahnenerbe," in: Hauschild, 168 ff., the tabulated comparisons with assigned percentages are found in the foot notes.] The Atlantis ideas cultivated by

occult-satanic background of the Russian revolution and last but not least, in the face of his agreement with the claims of Baron von der Osten-Sacken about a supposed activity of "secret organizations, which sent their threads from a secret center at the farthest distance"[1] and his familiarity with de Mengel's commentary about the "Black-Center," it is plausible that Himmler was not only interested in contents transported in occult circles, but truly shared the belief in a shortly to occur dualistic-gnostic-coined, apocalyptic final battle between the occult center of the white magicians on one side and the center of the black magicians on the other. The existence of such a world view is, to us, far beyond all accessible explanation models of the world today, and substantially shifts, in my opinion, the perspective of Himmler's motivations with reference to the persecution of Freemasons and Jews.

---

the Polars, were just as much maintained in the German-speaking occult milieu and are therefore not exclusive of the Polaires: [see Wegener, AWB] The theosophically-inspired Ariosoph, Chancellor of the Edda Society and brother in Lanzen's order [Mohler, 355], Rudolf Gorsleben (1883-1930), wrote: "All indication show that life on Earth ... arose at the north pole, therefore also man. When the polar region cooled and became inhospitable, mankind spread ray-like from the pole across the entire Earth ... After its shifting from the pole, the sunken world of Atlantis became the center of post-polar humanity which is counted with the fourth root-race of the Atlanter and the secret teachings [of Blavatsky]. The following 5th root-race [root-race is a term also used by Steiner – see Wegener, Schuler, 60 ff.] of Aryans is the main inheritor of the slowly perishing Atlantan root-race ... The common origin of all Arian mythologies from the Arian ur-religion, once included in all rites of the contemporary divine services, was thought very much as being common intuition that it was not further discussed ..." [Gorsleben, 58 f.] That Himmler possibly searched in Tibet also for the survivors of the cosmic catastrophe, mentioned by Maurice Magre, who were supposed to have survived the destruction of Atlantis follows from the memoirs of a participant in the Tibet expedition. According to it Himmler stated: "There are still numerous remnants of the tertiary moon people, the last witnesses of the disappeared, once world-encompassing Atlantis culture. In Peru, for instance, on Easter Island and, as I assume, in Tibet." [citing Sünner, 48. Sünner on his source in the matter of the Tibet-Atlantis relationship: "Unfortunately, I cannot tell you anything more specific to this point, since I promised the person who made the memoirs available to me that I would not publicly mention the author. This was the requirement to sight the Wiligut passages from the autobiography. I keep such promises and ask for your understanding. I can only say that I checked the source which appears reasonable to me." [Mail Sünner-Wegener of May 26, 2004]]

1   Osten-Sacken, 55

**Himmler collected newspaper clipping, among which was this advertisement:**

"Section of the famous map of the insiders (puppet masters) from the year 1890 ...
That all was to have been planned already in 1890? There were to have been people who
– determined in advance that, at the time Kaiser Wilhelm was pushed abroad ...
– East Prussia was separated by the Polish corridor from Danzig to Upper Silesia!
– Russia became a desert, a ransacked country! ...

Yes, the map was copied in 1890 in the periodical 'Truth' of the High-grade insider, Mister Labouchère (London, Christmas issue). How may the 300 inside men who, following Rathenau's remark, have guided destiny (from the background!), and have smiled when they had a look at this map! How every single one then worked in his position to bring this map to its fulfillment,
– how the World War was required for it and was triggered, ...
– how then the Jewry of the world fell upon the Central Powers with the help of the Marxists, paid and led by the Jews, to depose the Tzar, and to cause Germany's collapse ..."

[BArch, Nachlass Himmler, N 1126, NL 126/5]

# 9 Afterword

Spiritualism/Occultism doubtlessly experienced its high point at the Fin de Siècle, towards the end of the 19th century. Then, its star quickly faded in the face of the increasing calls for scientific methodology which, by that time, had sufficiently demonstrated its function. Since the 19th century, meticulous experiments had exposed much of the ghostly going-ons as fraudulent. In so doing, many of the old, since classical times, traditional wisdoms were taken to their grave by empirical experiments in the laboratory. The end of the ether was also sealed in this way. William Butler Yeats, the Irish Nobel-prize winner in literature, described such an experiment in his autobiography: "In one of the books or journals published by the [Theosophical] Society, there had appeared a quotation from an essay on magic by an author of the seventeenth century, stating that, if one incinerates a flower to ashes and puts it, I believe, under the tank of an air pump, after which one puts the tank for so-and-so-many nights into moonlight, then the spirit of the flower would appear and hover above its ashes. I appointed a committee which performed this experiment without any result."[1]

When Heinrich Himmler started his occult carrier at the beginning of the 1920s, the star of the once innovative and potential occultism[2] had long since faded, which is why to him that could only apply to what zur Bonsen had expressed in 1923:

"The tendency for the secretive, the love for excitement, the creepy, is, in any case, in the people's blood, and what, in this respect, can be observed plenty of times, especially in children – not to mention the ill, feverish boy of Goethe's Erlkönig –, applies oftentimes, more or less, to adults with a narrow outlook and education. Yes, and not only to those!"[3]

With the establishment of the Ahnenerbe, a field opened to Himmler to further deepen his early tendencies. The competitive situation with Alfred Rosenberg, who plowed a similar field, and biting, polemic criticism from the camp of the scholarly sciences forced him eventually to distance himself, little

---

1 Yeats, 186
2 Acc. to Eduard Wildhagen Rudolf Hess had striven in the first years of the Third Reich for a foundation capital of 12 million marks and an annual subvention of 2 million for a planned "Central Institute for Occultism." [Heiber, 806; Ger. Fed. Arch. Z 42 IV/3512a fol. 86]
3 Bonsen, 77

by little, from his dubious occult advisors and their subjects. The possible discovery of his SS-Brigadeleader Wiligut's past spent in an insane asylum, could have evolved into a PR-disaster for the entire movement.[1] The purposeful and rational working-off of the proceedings about the Epidemic Witch Nasav at the height of the war indicate however, that, at this point in time, even such downfields for an imaginary, new SS-hokuspokus were no longer taken up. Anyway, the 'right' people were not available. But it would certainly be wrong to conclude automatically from the termination of most occult activities at the war's beginning on a change-of-heart of Himmler. To my knowledge, Himmler's verifiable occupation with occult subjects began in 1921 with his reading of "The Dead are alive," and ended, by no means, at the beginning of the war. Even in August of 1943 Himmler dispatched the dowser [!] Josef Wimmer to search for a "legendary treasure" in the Hohenhöwen Mountain, a basalt peak in the Hegau. Wimmer was to locate gold there with his divining rod.[2]

The search for gold by means of a divining rod, the wish to obtain gold with the aid of a "Gold maker," the search for Mussolini's hiding place through astrologers, the connection of political actions to moon constellations – all this confirms Himmler's bent for the occult even long past the beginning of the war. One can therefore not speak with reference to Himmler, of a temporary eccentricity or a youthful diversion. Rather it must have been a firmly anchored line of thought which represented one of the foundations of Himmler's way of dealing with reality. However, decisions made on the basis of a possible influence on reality by will (magic), had, in most cases, to be wrong. A scientific opponent, unable to go along with Himmler's and Hitler's belief in the destruction of Atlantis by an impact of the moon on the Earth (the so-called "World-Ice-doctrine"), described the problem in 1938 as follows: For Germany's standing, "The World-Ice doctrine is a deeply regrettable relapse into the long overcome primitive early stage of scientific research, dominant in the early Middle Ages ... It is characteristic for the World-Ice doctrine to reject the results of experiments and observation and is based on a purely imaginary world view ..."[3] The

---

1   In 1939 Wiligut's department was dissolved after his history of illness became known. [Lange, Wiligut, 70] This did not prevent Himmler at all to still meet with Wiligut on November 28, 1941. [Himmler, Dienstkalender, 276]
2   Kater, 222. The "Research Department for the Checking of the so-called Secret Sciences" did not only exist in 1939 but still in 1943/44. [Kater, Schaubilder Organization Ahnenerbe, Attachment] For the dowser Wimmer see also: Himmler, Dienstkalender, 413, 523.
3   Letter of Prof. Paul Guthnick to the Reichsminister for Science, Education, and People's Education of 1938, Germ. Fed. Arch.NS 19-1705, page 53 f., see also Wegener, AWB,

"purely imaginary construct" of reality sprang from magical thinking which continuously traded reality with fiction and was already thought antiquated at the turn of the century. This was nothing of concern – as long as the supporters of these magical thought structures had no executive powers. But Himmler possessed precisely those, after he had been washed to power by the waves of the gnostic revolution, long since prepared for by Romantic and German Idealism. And not all hokuspokus that washed across the German-French border into the Reichl was occult. Behind the deepest irrational methods hid, in most cases, gnosis – which had to be taken seriously as an old antagonist of Catholicism.

The camouflaged attack proceeded simultaneously on multiple fronts: Behind the façade of modern genetics hid a biologically-turned race gnosticism; behind the backdrop of the supposed new-heathen groups in Germany waited the German people for their deification and even such physically-appearing theories of the occult scene as the "Od," last not least, carried only the old *pleroma* (Abundance of Light) across the gnostic home stretch. The optics deceived: The religious part of National-Socialism was no motley collection of contradictory approaches and methods, but an eruption of a centuries-long, under Europe's Christian cover continuing, forgotten religio-philosophial current: the gnosis. It formed the core around which the growing political religion of National-Socialism positioned itself for the final battle against the 'Powers of Darkness' – only to lose again to reality. Himmler's possible belief in deceased warlords (Heinrich I) and black magicians (Heise), acting secretly from the beyond, further enriched the gnostic scenario with a starkly dualistic component. The image of the sunken island served as a draw: Pulled by the image of an imaginary paradise of pure-light, blond-eyed Aryans, settled in a secular version of the gnostic *pleroma* (Abundance of Light), Atlantis, Himmler was simultaneously pushed in his behavior: Repelled by a vision of occult, black forces and the gnostic god of darkness he moved into the direction of war.

In occult circles – such must be reconstructed – this kind of conspiracy scenario must have, more or less, been maintained: Behind the Freemasons and Jews were hiding their "Brothers of the Chair" and other group leaders. These were supposedly steered by the representatives of an occult brotherhood, the "Dark Mahatmas" (according to Martinist-Order-opinion / Theosophy / Guénon), who, as far as they were concerned, were again supposedly centrally instructed from a "Black-Center" of undetermined location on Earth. (Osten-

Sacken / de Mengel / Klages¹) It's head, the Black Magus (Schuler) is already an entity with supernatural powers mediating between the worldly and the otherworldly (Marquès-Rivière). Its agents, for instance, become intoxicated by the supernatural Fluidum ("murder-blood-light") flowing from the blood of the freshly killed (Heise/Schuler), and receive advice from the realm of the dead (Heise/Steiner). The "Angels of Darkness" (Marquès-Rivière) must be placed above the Black Magus. They perform the classic mediation role of angels – to the gnostic adversary of light, the god of darkness.

Thus, in 1925, the Protestant pastor, Richard Hannuschka, saw the "Prince of Darkness", a "God", act behind the Jews and Freemasons: "The 'God' of the Jews ... was not our God, he was the spirit of darkness, the Devil himself." "Since no explanation on Freemasonry can be found in any textual material ... what constitutes the 'Council of Seven' is, is said herewith. It no longer is about human beings who exercise this power, but about ... spiritual beings which make themselves known through mediums ... Mircha has the power of materialization ... and is ... the Prince of Darkness." The "systematic mass murders of Soviet Jews in Russia" are to him blood sacrifices, ritual murders, which the Jews were bringing their "Lord and Master, the Devil."²

This god is rarely mentioned, but his existence can be inferred by the existence of mediating beings, the angels of darkness. As of today, there are theoretical conspiracy texts that recapitulate this theological subject of a hierarchy of occult lodges all the way up to Lucifer/Satan, even by reverting to sources of the 20s,

---

1   The philosopher Ludwig Klages, whose mentor was Schuler, wrote in 1940: " ... The fact is that actually already since Christianity's victory ... the warlike as well as unwarlike changes within Christianity, and thus within the prevailing part of earthly residents occurred essentially by plan, more specifically under the leadership of hidden power centers with a character hostile to life. The obviously (manifest) human history, we may say briefly, was to some extent brought to daylight with the revelation of the secret (latent) one is presently occupied and that not without success ... Must we say that from the hidden power centers the strings gather at one and only one center? ... Barely for the German of the present, as far as he gives the power center appropriately the name Juda." [Klages, Ludwig: "Einführung des Herausgebers," in: Schuler, Fragmente, 43] Klages, too, does not deal only with earthly power struggles, but at root with a metaphysical aspect: "The history of mankind shows us now in mankind, and only in mankind, the fight 'to the death' between the widespread life and an extra-space-time power, which turn the oles against each other and thus destroy them, take the soul from the body, the body from the soul: it is called the spirit (Logos, Pneuma, Nus)." [Klages, Eros, 64] An extra-space-time power, a power beyond the known space and time realm, must be a metaphysical power, of which Klages writes. [see also Wegener, Schuler, 93]

2   Hannuschka, 42, 25, 76, 82

30s, and 40s, as per Wolfgang Eggert, who, in the chapter "Bolshevism – Zionism – Freemasonry" in his publication "Israel's Secret Vatican" in the paragraph title "Br. Kerenski – Governor of Power," addresses also Kerenski as treated by Heise.[1]

I began this book with the fearful, visionary short story "The Caftan" by Kurt Münzer, which appeared in 1915 in a collection titled "The Ghost War." In 1922, Himmler was seriously disappointed following his reading of "The Ghost War." He commented: "The title promises something different. These are simply peculiar events from the war ..."[2] Following the above comments, the question what Himmler expected from the title "Ghost War" instead, can now more easily be answered: A representation of the battle of hidden forces in the realm of the dead and beyond.

I must therefore contradict Bradley Smith who, in his examination[3] of Himmler's childhood and youth arrived at the conclusion: "Heinrich Himmler's career as a professional National-Socialist was the product of a slow personal development that was neither irrational nor demonic. To the challenges posed by the revolutionary changes that shook the traditional societal institutions to the beginning of the first World War, he answers that it was an attempt to adjust the old values and schemata to the new requirements."[4] Actually, Himmler's development before the time background within which he moved, can be reconstructed. Nevertheless, his belief in occult power centers goes far beyond the, by no means, atypical games of the time with spiritual subjects and occult motives. No, Himmler's development was by no means "demonic," but – measured against his contemporaries – was quite irrational.

"National-Socialism and Occultism" is also the subject of Hakl's overview. He relativizes the diverse theories about the occult tendencies in National-Socialism and writes about Himmler: "His addressed esoteric tendencies were his private

---

1   Eggert, Wolfgang: "Israels Geheimvatikan, " Vol. 2, 2. Publ. Munich 2002, 237, 302
2   Himmler's commentary to "Der Gespensterkrieg" continues with the words "... and the War time which, in part, that is I and II [this does not refer to Münzer's short story], as much as possible incomprehensibly dressed up and told" [Himmler, Reading list, Title entry no. 125, page 16] Stutterheim: "[The 'Dritte Reich'] is based nevertheless on a patchwork of occult teachings and myths ... The frequently thematicized and presented belief in the own electedness, unconditional obedience, and faithfulness of the adherents, as well as the generation of a special doctrine of world-connections, produce an image of a sect that attained political power." [Stutterheim, 156]
3   Smith deals only briefly in three places in his examination of Himmler's youth with Himmler's fascination with occult subjects. [Smith, Weg, 145, 194, 213]
4   Smith, Weg, 224

matter and were not taken seriously in important circles." A position he repeats in his exposition about Hess: "But here, too, as with Himmler, private interests are at stake that have nothing to do with his political position."[1] As a result of the presented examinations, it can be said that these evaluations with respect to Himmler are wrong: If Himmler's image of the enemy with respect to Freemasonry and Jews was fed also by occult patterns, one can no longer speak of a "private matter," since the political and, by no means, private consequence of Himmler's occult world view must be called mass murder.

---

[1] Hakl, H. T., Article: Afterword, in: Goodrick-Clarke, Nicholas: "Die okkulten Wurzeln des Nationalsozialismus," Graz 1997, 194, 197, 199. Stutterheim also arrives at a different assessment: "Heinrich Himmler, in the circle of leading Nationalsocialists, is the one who most strongly subscribed to occult images, supported them publicly and let them enter into his actions and speeches." [Stutterheim, 144]

```
SS-Brigadeführer                  Berlin SW 68, den 28.6.1937.
K.M. Weisthor                     Bodemannstr. 23/24.
B.A. III 2309/a/468.
L./Schb.

                    G e h e i m !

    Betr.: Nachricht von Herrn Gaston de M e n g e l aus Helsinki.
    Bezug: ---
    Anlg.: ---

                An den
                R e i c h s f ü h r e r   SS
                Chef des Persönlicher Stab
                SS-Gruppenführer  W o l f f
                B e r l i n    SW 11
                ---------------------
                Prinz Albrecht Str.

    In einem höchst geheimnisvoll gehaltenen Schreiben vom
    23.6.37 aus Helsinki macht mir Herr Gaston de M e n g e l
    eine merkwürdige Mitteilung. Er schreibt etwa folgendes:

    " Die Achse, die nord-östlich von Paris liegt, arbeitet
    sehrsstark. Doch liegt die Achse weder bei Berlin noch
    bei Helsinki. Ich habe aus dem Durchschnitt der Achse
    den Ausgangspunkt der Kräfte bestimmen können. Er liegt
    in Murm (Lappland) etwa 35° östl. Länge und 68° nördl.
    Breite in der Umgebung des Lowosero in Rußland. Ich
    habe auch den Ort von dem großen Schwarz-Zentrum be-
    stimmt. Er liegt innerhalb des großen Dreiecks, das von
    Kobdo, Urumtschi und Bakul gebildet wird, bei Sin-kiang
    in der westl. Mogolei. "

    Ich bringe dieses Schreiben deshalb zur Kenntnis, weil
    Gaston de Mengel mich fragt, was ich davon halte.-Ich
    halte diese Information für immerhin beachtenswert und
    bitte ihr entsprechende Aufmerksamkeit zu schenken.

    Meiner Vermutung nach werden dort von den Russen nach
    Übereinkunft mit Frankreich und England Flugstützpunkte
    errichtet. Ob diese Vermutung zutrifft, könnte der SD
    zu ergründen versuchen.

                                            SS-Brigadeführer
```

„höchst geheimnisvoll" ("most arcane") –
even Himmler's chief occultist Wiligut did not know what to make of it (Ger. Fed. Arch.)

# 10 Bibliography

Ackerman, Josef: Himmler als Ideologe, Göttingen 1970

André, Marie-Sophie; Beaufils, Christophe: Papus biographie – la Belle Epoque de l'occultisme, Paris 1995

BArch / Bundesarchiv / German Federal Archives : http://www.bundesarchiv.de/

Behler, Ernst: Die Ewigkeit der Welt, München 1965, cit. Behler, Welt

Behler, Ernst, article: Ewigkeit der Welt, in: Ritter, Joachim u.a. (Hrsg.): Historisches Wörterbuch der Philosophie, Darmstadt 1972, Bd. 2, 846

Besgen, Achim: Der stille Befehl – Medizinalrat Kersten und das Dritte Reich, München 1960

Bhotiva, Zam: Asia Mysteriosa – L'Oracle de Force Astrale comme moyen de communication avec 'Les Petits Lumières d'Orient' – Précédé d'une préface de F. Divoire et d'études par Maurice Magre et J. Marquès-Rivière, Paris 1929

Bonsen, Friedrich zur: Das Zweite Gesicht (Die „Vorgeschichten") – Nach Wirklichkeit und Wesen, neue Ausgabe, Essen 1940

Brumlik, Micha: Die Gnostiker, Frankfurt/M. 1992

Bundesarchiv / German Federal Archives: http://www.bundesarchiv.de

Cooke, Ivan; Eagle, White: Vom Wirken der weißen Bruderschaft – Die Geschichte der White Eagle Gemeinschaft, Germering 1997 [Introduction: Colum Hayward]

Daim, Wilfried: Der Mann, der Hitler die Ideen gab. Jörg Lanz von Liebenfels, 3. edition, Wien 1994

Dörrie, Heinrich, article: Platon, in: Kleiner Pauly, Bd. 4

Encausse, Gérard Anaclet-Vincent: La Pensée – son mécanisme et son action, Nice 1921

Evola, Julius: Das Mysterium des Grals, München 1955, cit. Evola, Gral

Evola, Julius: Erhebung wider die moderne Welt, Stuttgart 1935, cit. Evola, Erhebung

Evola, Julius: Grundrisse der faschistischen Rassenlehre, Berlin 1943, cit. Evola, Rassenlehre

Evola, Julius: Heidnischer Imperialismus, Leipzig (Armanen-Verlag) 1933, cit. Evola, Imperialismus

Fidler, Matthias: Die Toten leben! Wirkliche Tatsachen über das persönliche Fortleben nach dem Tode, 2. edition, Leipzig, Verlag von Max Spohr, 1909

Fritsch, Theodor: Handbuch der Judenfrage – Die wichtigsten Tatsachen zur Berurteilung des jüdischen Volkes, 41. edition, 215000-225000, Leipzig 1937

Gastin, Louis: Comment on Entre dans la Société Théosophique – Comment on en Sort, Contribution à l'histoire de la S.T. – Précisions relatives à son Doctrine et à son pseudo-libéralisme, Avec une lettre de M. Albert Jounet, Bibliotheque Hermétique du Sud-Est; 49, Rue Montaux; Marseille 1919

German Federal Archives / Bundesarchiv / BArch: http://www.bundesarchiv.de

Glowka, Hans Jürgen: Deutsche Okkultgruppen 1875-1937, München 1981

Godwin, Joscelyn: Arktos – the polar myth, Grand Rapids (USA) 1993

Gorsleben, Rudolf John: Hoch-Zeit der Menschheit – Das Welt-Gesetz der Drei oder Entstehen-Sein-Vergehen in Ursprache-Urschrift-Urglaube. Aus den Runen geschöpft, Leipzig 1930

Grassi, Ernesto (Hrsg.): Platon – Sämtliche Werke, Hamburg 1987

Großheim, Michael (Hrsg.): Perspektiven der Lebensphilosophie – Zum 125. Geburtstag von Ludwig Klages, Bonn 1999, cit. Großheim, Perspektiven

Gruschke, Andreas: Die heiligen Stätten der Tibeter – Mythen und Legenden von Kailash bis Shambhala, München 1997

Guénon, René: Der König der Welt, München 1956 (1926), cit. Guénon, König

Guénon, René: Études sur la Franc-Maçonnerie et le Compagnonnage, Tome I, Éditions Traditionnelles („successeurs de la Maison ‚Chacornac'"), Paris 2000

Guénon, René: Le Théosophisme – Histoire d'une pseudo-religion, Reprint Paris 1982 (1921)

Gutman, Israel (Hrsg.): Enzyklopädie des Holocaust - Die Verfolgung und Ermordung der europäischen Juden, Bd. I-IV, München 1998

Hagen, Walter [i.e. SS-Obersturmbannführer Dr. Wilhelm Höttl]: Unternehmen Bernhard. Ein historischer Tatsachenbericht über die größte Geldfälschungsaktion aller Zeiten, Wels und Starnberg 1955

Hannuschka, Richard: Hinter der Maske der Freimaurerei, Berlin-Schöneberg 1935

Hauschild, Thomas (Hrsg.): Lebenslust und Fremdenfurcht – Ethnologie im Dritten Reich, Frankurt/M. 1995

Heiber, Helmut: Walter Frank und sein Reichsinstitut für Geschichte des neuen Deutschlands, Stuttgart 1966

Heise, Karl: Okkultes Logentum, Zürich 1921

Hergemöller, Bernd-Ulrich: Krötenkuss und schwarzer Kater – Ketzerei, Götzendienst und Unzucht in der inquisitorischen Phantasie des 13. Jahrhunderts, Warendorf 1996

Hieronimus, Ekkehard: Lanz von Liebenfels – Eine Bibliographie, Toppenstedt 1991

Himmler, Heinrich: Der Dienstkalender Heinrich Himmlers 1941/42, Hamburg 1999, cit. Himmler, Dienstkalender

Himmler, Heinrich: Leseliste 1919-1934, Bundesarchiv (BArch), Nachlass Himmler, Bestand N 1126, NL 126/9, fol. 1, übertragen von Ludwig Krieger 1966, cit. Himmler, Leseliste

Himmler, Katrin: Die Brüder Himmler. eine deutsche Familiengeschichte, 2. edition Oktober 2005 [107, 121, 164]

Howe, Ellic: Uranias Kinder, Weinheim 1995

Jacob, Frank (Ed.): Secret Societies: Comparative Studies in culture, society and history, Würzburg 2013

Jürgens, Heinrich: Pendelpraxis und Pendelmagie : Anl. zum Gebr. des siderischen Pendels zwecks Feststellung von Krankheiten u. menschl. Charaktereigenschaften, Geschlechtsbestimmg u. Befragung der Jenseitigen, Pfullingen i. Wtt. [1925]

Kater, Michael H.: Das „Ahnenerbe" der SS 1935-1945, 3. edition, München 2001

Kersten, Felix: Totenkopf und Treue – Heinrich Himmler ohne Uniform – Aus den Tagebüchern des finnischen Medizinalrats Felix Kersten, Hamburg 1953

Kettler, Sabine; Stuckel, Eva-Maria; Wegener, Franz: Wer tötete Helmut Daube – Der bestialische Sexualmord an dem Schüler Helmut Daube im Ruhrgebiet 1928, Gladbeck 2001

Klages, Ludwig (Hrsg.): Schuler, Alfred: Fragmente und Vorträge aus dem Nachlass. Mit einer Einführung von Ludwig Klages, Leipzig 1940, cit. Klages, Fragmente

Klages, Ludwig: Vom Kosmogonischen Eros. 2. edition, Jena 1926, cit. Klages, Eros

Köhler, J., article: Schöpfung, in: Ritter, Joachim u.a. (Hrsg.): Historisches Wörterbuch der Philosophie, Bd. 8, Basel 1992, Sp. 1389f., cit. Köhler

Kotowski, Elke-Vera: Feindliche Dioskuren. Theodor Lessing und Ludwig Klages – Das Scheitern einer Jugendfreundschaft (1885-1899), Berlin 2000

Krabbe, Wolfgang: Gesellschaftsveränderung durch Lebensreform – Strukturmerkmale einer sozialreformerischen Bewegung im Deutschland der Industrialisierungsperiode, Göttingen 1974

Lange, Hans-Jürgen: Otto Rahn und die Suche nach dem Gral, Engerda 1999, cit. Lange, Rahn

Lange, Hans-Jürgen: Weisthor. Karl-Maria Wiligut – Himmlers Rasputin und seine Erben, Engerda 1998, cit. Lange, Wiligut

Lindenberg, Christoph: Rudolf Steiner – Eine Biographie, Band II, 1915-1925, Verlag Freies Geistesleben, Stuttgart 1997, cit. Lindenberg, Biographie, II

Lindenberg, Christoph: Rudolf Steiner – Eine Chronik. 1861-1925, Verlag Freies Geistesleben, Stuttgart 1988, cit. Lindenberg, Chronik

Longerich, Peter: Heinrich Himmler. Biographie, München 2010

Lorenz, Sönke u.a. (Hrsg.): Himmlers Hexenkartothek. Das Interesse des Nationalsozialismus an der Hexenverfolgung. (Hexenforschung Bd. 4), 2. edition, Bielefeld 2000

Magre, Maurice: La Clef des Choses Cachées, Paris 1935

Marquès-Rivière, Jean [i.e. Jean Marie Rivière]: A l'Ombre des Monastères Thibétains – Preface des Maurice Magre, Paris et Neuchatel 1929

Mengel, Gaston de, article: Die Krisis des Musikalischen und dramatischen Unterrichts, in „Vivre", Nr. 5, 15. Juli 1926; Nr. 6 15. August und so weiter bis Nr. 13, 15. März 1927 – unbeendet

Mengel, Gaston de, article: Die Sinnbildlichkeit der Dreieinigkeit, in "Bulletin des Polaires", Mai, Juni, Juli, August 1932

Mengel, Gaston de, article: Knowledge and Immortality, in: Review of philosophy and religion, Vol. IV, Nr. 1, März 1933, Aryabhushan Press, Poona, Indien, S. 32ff.

Mengel, Gaston de, article: L'archéologie de l'Atlantide (d'après Lewis Spencer) , in: Voile d'Isis, 1931/513

Mengel, Gaston de, article: L'ésotérisme de la Musique, in: Voile d'Isis, 1928/483

Mengel, Gaston de: L'Ésotérisme de la musique [book], Paris 1929

Mengel, Gaston de, article: L'Infidelité des Francs-Maçons, in "Mercure de France", Série Moderne, 1. Juli – 1. August 1935, 310ff:

Mengel, Gaston de, article: Le Chant de la Vie, in: Voile d'Isis, 1929/444

Mengel, Gaston de, article: Le Pourquoi et le Comment de l'Education Physique, in "Penser et Agir" 3/4, 1926, 113ff.

Mengel, Gaston de, article: La notion de l'Absolu dans diverses formes de la Tradition, in: Voile d'Isis, 1929/384

Mengel, Gaston de, article: Le Ternaire dans le Manifesté, in: Voile d'Isis, (1) 1930/157

Mengel, Gaston de, article: Le Ternaire dans le Manifesté, in: Voile d'Isis, (2) 1930/356

Mengel, Gaston de, article: La Trinité et son oeuvre créatrice dans diverses formes", in: Voile d'Isis, (1) 1929/634

Mengel, Gaston de, article: La Trinité et son oeuvre créatrice dans diverses formes, in: Voile d'Isis, (2) 1929/700

Mengel, Gaston de, article: La Trinité et son oeuvre créatrice dans diverses formes, in: Voile d'Isis, (3) 1929/766

Mengel, Gaston de, article: Les éléments traditionnels dans le Gnosticisme, in: Voile d'Isis, 1930/691

Mengel, Gaston de, article: Quelques aspects de la Shakti, in: Voile d'Isis, 1931/732

Mengel, Gaston de: Skript der Vorlesung Juli/August 1929 im amerikanischen Konversatorium und in der Schule der bildenden Künste im Palast Fontainbleau: Die Prinzipien der allgemeinen Ästhetik [concerning François del Sarte – acc. Quellverzeichnis Ahnenerbe, BArch NS19-3974, Blatt 18-28, Schlarb an Himmler v. 26.4.1937 „Arbeiten des Herrn de Mengel"]

Mengel, Gaston de, article: The evidence for authentic transmutation, in: „The Journal of the Alchemical Society, edited by H. Stanley Redgrove, Nr. 1, (3 Volumes), 1913-1915

Mengel, Gaston de, article: The philosophical channels of alchemical tradition, in: „The Journal of the Alchemical Society, edited by H. Stanley Redgrove, Nr. 3, (3 Volumes), 1913-1915

Meyer, Brün (Hrsg.): Dienstaltersliste der Schutzstaffel der NSDAP (SS), Stand vom 1. Dezember 1938 mit Berichtigungsheft: Stand vom 15. Juni

1939, bearbeitet von der SS-Personalkanzlei, Unveränderter Nachdruck der Ausgaben Berlin 1938 und 1939, Osnabrück 1996

Mirbt, Carl: Quellen zur Geschichte des Papsttums und des römischen Katholizismus, 4. edition, Tübingen 1924

Mohler, Armin. Die Konservative Revolution in Deutschland 1918-1932 – Ein Handbuch, 4. edition, Darmstadt 1994, cit. Mohler

Müller, Baal [i.e. Müller, Karsten] (Hrsg,): Alfred Schuler: Cosmogonische Augen. Gesammelte Schriften, herausgegeben, kommentiert und eingeleitet von Baal Müller, Paderborn 1997, cit. Müller, „Augen"

Müller, Reiner: Deutschlands Abwehr chemischer oder bakteriologischer Angriffe, Köln 1933

Müller, Reiner: Lehrbuch der Hygiene für Ärzte und Biologen, München 1935

Müller, Reiner: Medizinische Mikrobiologie – Parasiten, Bakterien, Immunität, 3. edition, Berlin 1946

Oesterreich, Traugott Konstantin: Der Okkultismus im modernen Weltbild, Dresden 1921

Oehler, Klaus: Der Unbewegte Beweger des Aristoteles, Frankfurt 1984

Osmont, Anne: Mes souvenirs – 50 années d'occultisme – Mes voyages en astral, Paris 1941

Ossendowski, Ferdinand: Tiere, Menschen und Götter, 81.-90. Tausend, Frankfurt 1924

Padfield, Peter: Himmler – Reichsführer-SS, London 2001

Prel, Carl du: Der Spiritismus, Leipzig 1922

Rahn, Otto: Kreuzzug gegen den Gral, Freiburg im Breisgau 1933

Rahn, Otto: Luzifers Hofgesind, Leipzig 1937

Reiss, Tom: Der Orientalist. Auf den Spuren von Essad Bey, München 2010

Rudolph, Enno (Hrsg.): Zeit, Bewegung, Handlung – Studien zur Zeitabhandlung des Aristoteles, Stuttgart 1988, 111, cit. Rudolph

Sabah, Lucien: Une police politique de Vichy: le Service des Sociétés Secrètes, Paris 1996

Saint-Yves d'Alveydre, Alexandre: Mission de l'Inde en Europe – Mission de l'Europe en Asie, Reprint Nice 1981

Schmitz, Peter: Die Artamanen - Landarbeit und Siedlung bündischer Jugend in Deutschland 1924-1935, Bad Neustadt a. d. Saale 1985

Schmude, Detlef, article: „Ariosophische Gedichte und Sprüche", in: Reichstein, Herbert (Hrsg.): Ariosophische Bibliothek. Bücherei für ariogermanische Selbsterkenntnis, Heft 6, Düsseldorf-Unterrath [1926], cit. Schmude, Gedichte

Sède, Gérard de: Rennes-le-Château – Le dossier, les impostures, les phantasmes, les hypothèses, Paris 1988

See, Klaus von: Barbar Germane Arier – Die Suche nach der Identität der Deutschen, Heidelberg 1994

Smith, Bradley F. (Hrsg.): Heinrich Himmler – Geheimreden 1933 bis 1945 und andere Ansprachen, Frankfurt/M. 1974, cit. Smith

Smith, Bradley, F.: Heinrich Himmler 1900-1926. Sein Weg in den deutschen Faschismus, München, 1979, cit. Smith, Weg

Spiegel, Friedrich: Avesta – Die Heiligen Schriften der Parsen, Bd.1-3, Leipzig 1852-1863

Strunk, Johann: Zu Juda und Rom – Tibet. Ihr Ringen um die Weltherrschaft, München 1938

Stutterheim, Kerstin D.: Okkulte Weltvorstellungen im Hintergrund dokumentarischer Filme des „Dritten Reiches", Berlin 2000

Sünner, Rüdiger: Schwarze Sonne – Entfesselung und Missbrauch der Mythen im Nationalsozialismus und rechter Esoterik, Freiburg i. Breisgau 1999

Trimondi, Victor u. Victoria [i.e. Röttgen, Herbert and Mariana]: Hitler, Buddha, Krishna – Eine unheilige Allianz vom Dritten Reich bis heute, Wien 2002

Viard, Marcel: Le Naturisme et la Guerre, Paris 1928

Waterfield, Robin: René Guénon and the Future of the West – The life and writings of a 20th-century metaphysician, Wellingborough 1987

Webb, James: The Occult Underground [19th century], La Salle, Illinois 1974, cit. Webb, Underground

Webb, James: The Occult Establishment [20th century], La Salle, Illinois 1976, cit. Webb, Establishment

Wegener, Franz: Alfred Schuler, der letzte deutsche Katharer – Nationalsozialismus, Gnosis und mystische Blutleuchte, Gladbeck 2003, cit. Wegener, Schuler

Wegener, Franz: Das atlantidische Weltbild – Nationalsozialismus und Neue Rechte auf der Suche nach der versunkenen Atlantis, 2. edition, Gladbeck, 2003, cit. Wegener, AWB

Wegener, Franz: Der Alchemist Franz Tausend. Alchemie und Nationalsozialismus, Gladbeck 2006

Wegener, Franz: Gnosis in High Tech und Science-Fiction, Gladbeck 2009

Wegener, Franz: Kelten, Hexen, Holocaust: Menschenopfer in Deutschland, Gladbeck 2004, cit. Wegener, Kelten

Wegener, Franz: Memetik – Der Krieg des neuen Replikators gegen den Menschen, Gladbeck 2001

Wegener, Franz: Neu-Vineta. Die Rassesiedlungspläne der Ariosophen für die Halbinseln Darß und Zingst, Gladbeck 2010

Wegener, Franz: Weishaar und der Geheimbund der Guoten. Ariosophie und Kabbala, Gladbeck 2005

Wegner, Bernd: Hitlers politische Soldaten: die Waffen-SS 1933-1945: Leitbild, Struktur und Funktion einer nationalsozialistischen Elite, 3. edition, Paderborn 1988

Wilhelm, Hans-Heinrich u. Jong, Louis de: Zwei Legenden aus dem Dritten Reich : quellenkritische Studien, Stuttgart 1974

Worms, M.: Die Lehre von der Anfangslosigkeit der Welt bei den mittelalterlichen arabischen Philosophen des Orients und ihre Bekämpfung durch die arabischen Theologen, Bd. III., Heft IV, Münster 1900, cit. Worms

Wulff, Wilhelm: Tierkreis und Hakenkreuz – Als Astrologe an Himmlers Hof, Gütersloh 1968

Yeats, William Butler: Autobiografie, in: Vordtriede, Werner (Hrsg.): William Butler Yeats – Werke VI, Neuwied 1973

Zekl, Hans Günther: Aristoteles' Physik, Hamburg 1988, Bd. 2, cit. Zekl

# 11 Index

## A

Accomani, Cesare 120
Ackermann, Josef 19, 50, 52
Agrippa, Henricus Cornelius 18, 22
Ahasja 25
Ahriman 29
Ahura Mazda 29, 30, 31, 32, 54
Aksakow, Alexander 42, 44
Ammann, David 54
Anagarika 130
Andra 31
Antonie Gräfin zu 61
Argus 126
Aristotle 22, 43, 49, 82, 83, 84, 85
Arthur, King 56 f.
Asura 31
Avalon, Arthur 87

## B

Baal-Sebub 25
Barlaam 115
Barral, Jean 102
Batel, Fernand 101
Becquerel 37
Beder 30
Beelzebub 28
Beger 136
Bernadotte 51
Besgen, Achim 50f.
Bey, Essad 71
Beyle, Chultun 110
Bhikshu 83
Bhotiva, Zam 106, 108, 110, 117-124, 134
Binet, Alfred 82
Blanchard, Victor 105
Blavatsky, Helen 17, 49, 88, 104, 108, 111, 113, 137
Blech, Charles 103

Bolanden 88
Bonsen, Friedrich zur 52, 53, 56, 139
Boos-Jegher, Emma 135
Bopp, Franz 29
Borel, Pierre 102
Bormann, Martin 68
Bose, Fritz 92
Boullan, Abbé 102
Boumendil 108
Bourges, Elémir 103
Brandt 24, 25, 50
Breton 102
Brumlik, Micha 81
Brun, Charles 103
Bruno, Giordano 22
Buddha 30, 58, 104, 115, 129
Bülow, von 66
Burnof 113

## C

Çâkyamuni 30
Caligio) 21
Çarva 31
Chacornac, Paul 88
Charpentier 111
Chasshekankrakrya, Anagarika 129
Cherenski 129, 130, 131
Chesson, Lynn 3, 4
Clavelle, M. 81
Cohen, Kadmi 90
Combes, Léon 102
Conan Doyle, Sir Arthur 124
Cooke, Grace 124
Cooke, Ivan 124
Cromwell 56
Crookes, William 19
Crowley, Aleister 4, 99, 101

## D

Daiber, Albert Ludwig 88
D'Alviella, G. 113
Darré, Walther 65
Daudet, Alphonse 98
Daudet, Léon 98

David-Neel, Alexandra  89
De Jong  51
Demonforts, Michel  99
Descartes  82
Dessoir, Max  40
Dionysus Pseudo-Areopagita  86
Divoire, Fernand  108
D'Olivet, Fabre  108
Dönitz, Großadmiral  69
Dotzler  99
Doyle, Lady  124
Drukhs Naçus  31, 32
Durville  46

E

Eckstein, Friedrich  40
Eco, Umberto  90
Edison  58
Eggert, Wolfgang  143
Ekron  25, 28
Elgood, Cyril  31
Emmerick, Anna-Katharina  39, 116, 118
Encausse, Gérard (Papus)  16 f., 79, 97 f., 102, 105, 108, 134
Erebos  21
Eulenberg  12
Eulenburg, Antonie, Gräfin zu  61
Euripides  22
Eusapia  2
Evola  78, 113
Evola, Julius  113, 120

F

Farr, Florence  4
Faÿ, Bernard  126
Fechner, Gustav Theodor  19, 40
Feerhow, Friedrich  46
Feilgenhauer, Fritz  39
Ferrand, L.  102
Fest, Joachim  20
Fidler, Matthias  39, 41
Fille, Mario  120, 124, 125
Fleury, R.-A.  102
Fox, Katharina  37

Fox, Margaret  36
Frank, Walter  4
Friedrich  46, 88
Fritsch, Freiherr von  57
Fritsch, Theodor  54

G

Galen-Enniger  61
Gastin, Louis  101-105
Gates, Elmar  58
George, Stefan  21, 80
Ghengis Khan  110
Gibson, Mel  28
Glauer, Rudolf  88
Gobineau  28
Gobron, Gabriel  102
Godwin, Joscelyn  114, 125
Goethe  52, 139
Goodrick-Clarke, Nicholas  40
Gorsleben, Rudolf John  64-66, 137
Grawitz, Ernst  24, 25, 28, 33
Greve, Reinhard  136
Grialou, J.  102
Grönhagen, Yrjö von  91, 93, 131
Groth, Peter  39
Grünwedel, Albert  136
Guaita, Stanislas de  97, 102 f.
Guénon, René  57, 79, 90, 91, 113 f., 119, 120, 127, 141
Guthnick, Paul  140

H

Habel, Werner  4
Hakl, H. T.  143, 144
Hale, Christopher  136
Hanisch, Otto  54
Hanish, Zar-Adusht  54
Hannuschka, Richard  142
Hartmann, Eduard von  40, 44
Hartmann, Franz  99
Hartmann, Wilhelm  67
Hauer, Thomas  66
Hayward, Colum  123 f.
Heiber, Helmut  139

Heilmaier, Karl 59 ff.
Heise, Karl 55, 56, 57, 58, 130, 131, 134, 135 f., 141, 142, 143
Heise, Heinrich 55
Hellenbach von Paczoloy, Lazar Baron 40, 43
Helmont, Johannes Baptista Van 86
Henry, King 50 f., 141
Hergemöller, Bernd-Ulrich 17
Hertz 37
Hesiod 21, 22
Hess, Rudolf 67 f., 139, 144
Heydrich, Reinhard 68
Hieronimus 65
Himmler, Gebhard 15
Hitler, Adolf 19, 22, 23, 50, 70, 79, 140
Hoffet, Émile 97 f.
Home, Daniel 19
Homer 22
Hörmann, Dr. 68
Horus 119
Hübbe-Schleiden, Wilhelm 40
Huysmans 102
Hygin 21

I

Indra 31
Ishtar 87
Isis 87
Isnard, Daniel 102

J

Joasaph 115
Jobs, Steve 17
John, St. 124
Jollivet-Castelot, F. 102
Jones, Henry 97
Jones, William 17, 29
Joseph of Arimathia 77
Jounet, Albert 102, 103, 104
Julien, Brother 108
Julien, Father 110
Jung-Stilling, Johannes Heinrich 37 f., 52
Jupiter 30

Jürgens, Heinrich 44-50

K

Kamr essamans 30
Kant, Immanuel 40, 43, 82
Karbis 130
Kater, Michael 52, 68, 93
Keller, Comte Alexander 108
Keller, Comtesse 108
Kellner, Karl 99
Kerenski, Alexander 130 f., 143
Kersten, Felix 20, 47, 49, 50, 51, 57, 58, 68
Kettler, Sabine 4
Khrafçtras 32
Kiesewetter, Karl 40
Kirchhoff, Günther 127, 129
Klages, Ludwig 47, 142
Klein, Joshua 99
Krogh, Zene 3, 4
Kubin, Alfred 6
Kuhn, A. 32
Kurdzialek, Marian 22

L

Labouchère 138
Lachner, SS-Obersturmführer von 78 f., 94 ff.
Lange, Hans-Jürgen 23, 56, 57, 123, 129
Lanz, Adolf 63, 65, 69
Laurin, Stefan 4
Le Cour, Paul 102
Lehmann, Alfred 37
Le Leu, Louis 102
Lenin 130
Lepzet 17
Lienau, Walter 65, 66
Ligou 107
Lindenberg, Christoph 134 f.
Linné, Carl von 26
List, Guido 55
Lobbes 67
Loenartz 15
Lohalm 23
Lombroso, Cesare 42

Longerich, Peter 19
Lucas, Frank 4
Lucifer 142
Ludendorff, General von 131
Luraud 98
Lwoff 131

## M

Magre, Maurice 77, 106, 107, 108, 111, 112, 115 f., 120, 123, 137
Maitreya 30, 58, 129
Mani 29, 115
Marquès-Rivière, Jean 1, 101, 106, 108, 116 f., 120, 125-126, 136, 142
Masur, Norbert 70
Mathers, MacGregor 4
Maurras, Charles 98
Max Muller 113
Meister Eckhart 87
Melusson, G. 102
Mengel, Gaston de 78- 109, 127-142
Mesmer, Franz Anton 37 f., 45, 52
Meyer, Jul. 33
Miller, Alfred 20
Minesta 124
Mircha 142
Mohler, Armin 63
Molo, W. von 88
Moltke, Eliza von 135
Moltke, Helmuth von 135
Monti, Georges 95-99
Moritz, Lieutenant 125
Moses de Leon 81
Muhammad 49
Muller, Max 113
Müller, Reiner 25-33
Müller, SS-Standartenführer 62
Münzer, Kurt 6, 7, 143
Mussolini 67, 68, 78, 120, 140

## N

Nasav 31, 32, 34, 140
Nebe, Arthur 67
Nelson 56, 135

Neuberger, Helmut 88
Newton 22
Nogalès, Juan de 103
Nyx 21

## O

Oberhummer, E. 27
Odin 46
Odysseus 33
Osiris 56
Osmont, Anne 79, 98, 99
Ossendowski, Ferdinand 109 f., 114, 119, 134, 136
Osten-Sacken, Baron Gotthard von der 23, 71 f., 91, 137, 141
Oung Mong 129, 130

## P

Padfield, Peter 19, 52
Paehlke, Kurt 59, 62 f.
Paladino, Eusapia 42
Papus (see Encausse)
Paracelsus 22, 44
Pasqually, Martinès de 105
Pauen, Michael 47
Péladan 98, 103
Péladan, Joséphin 96, 98, 102
Penelope 33
Perisson, G. 102
Perraud, Raymond 102
Pfaffenzeller 61
Phaneg, G. 102
Piobb, Pierre 102
Pius IX 97
Plato 84, 85
Plinius 26
Plowzoff, Russian General 130
Podmore, Frank 1, 4
Pontikos, Kerakleides 22
Porphyrio 22
Porte-du-Trait-des-Ages, A. 102
Prel, Carl du 2, 40-43, 52 f., 85
Proklos 22
Prozor, Madame la Comtesse 103

Psellus 42

## Q

Quade, Fritz 46, 49

## R

Rahn, Max 40
Rahn, Otto 23, 76, 77, 78, 81, 91, 106, 107, 108, 115, 123
Rais, Gilles de 99
Ramin, Jürgen von 59
Rathenau, Walther 138
Reghini, Prof. 118
Reichenbach, Ludwig von 45 f.
Reuss, Theodor 99
Ritter, Joachim 22
Roca, Abbé 102
Röntgen, Conrad 37, 53
Rosenberg, Alfred 22, 78, 139
Ruhnau, Dietrich 63
Ruppmann, Kurt 79, 131, 133

## S

Sabah, Lucien 99
Saint Yves d'Alveydre, Alexandre 96, 105, 108 f., 114, 118f.
Saltzmann, Alphonse 102
Sâr Mérodak 103
Satan 142
Saunier, Jean 108
Scheffler 23
Schellenberg, Walter 56
Schiaparelli 42
Schlarb, Gertraut 79, 94 f., 131, 133
Schmid, Frenzolf 79, 88, 92
Schmude, Detlef 65
Schrenck-Notzing, Albert von 40
Schroeder, Werner 126
Schubert 136
Schuler, Alfred 21, 47, 50, 63, 134, 142
Schuré, Éduard 98
Schwartz-Bostunitsch, Gregor 88
Sebottendorf, Rudolf (von) 70, 88, 130

Sebregondi 52
Séde, Gérard de 94-101
Scholem, Gershom 81
Sievers, Wolfram 133, 136
Slade, Henry 19, 40
Smith, Bradley 143
Spengler, SS-Obersturmführer 63
Spiegel, Friedrich 29, 31, 32
Spielberg, Steven 77
Steiner, Rudolf 55, 134 f., 135, 137, 142
Stewart, Balfour 49
Stolberg-Wernigerode 61
Strömberg, Sven 40
Strunk, Johann 131
Stuckel, Eva-Maria 4
Stutterheim, Kerstin 18, 37, 40, 44, 49, 68, 69, 88, 118, 143, 144
Suchanek 68
Sünner, Rüdiger 137
Swedenborg, Emanuel 37, 38, 52, 116

## T

Tait, Peter Guthrie 49
Tappa 108
Tausend, Franz 68
Teudt, Wilhelm 129
Thomas, Saint 86
Thukydides 33
Trimondi (Röttgen, Herbert and Mariana) 20
Trotsky 130
Tyr 30

## U

Ungern-Sternberg, Baron von 109

## V

Vechi, Albert 103
Vella, Marcus 95, 97 f.
Viard, Marcel 101, 105, 107
Vulliaud, P. 113

## W

Waitz, Hans 81
Waterfield 114
Webb, James 4, 18, 19, 87, 97, 99, 102, 103, 105, 108
Wegner, Bernd 79
Wehofer, Friedrich 46
Weishaar (see Paehlke)
Westcott, Dr. Wynn 4
Wichtl, Friedrich 88
Wienert, Karl 136
Wilde, Oscar 1
Wilhelm, Kaiser 138
Wiligut, Karl-Maria 23, 51, 56, 78 f., 91, 127, 131-137, 140
Willermoz, J.-B. 105
Wimmer, Josef 140
Windolf, Herbert 3, 4
Winzer 94
Wirth, Oswald 102
Wolff, Karl 56, 78 f., 91, 93, 96, 133
Wulff, Veit 33
Wulff, Wilhelm 51, 67, 68 f.
Wüst, Walther 136

## Y

Yarker, John 99
Yeats, William Butler 1, 4, 105, 139

## Z

Zarathustra 25, 27, 29, 30, 31, 32
Zenon 22
Zeus 21, 30
Zoellner, C. F. 19

Made in the USA
Charleston, SC
03 July 2013